# 350 YEARS *of* NEW JERSEY HISTORY

## FROM STUYVESANT TO SANDY

Joseph G. Bilby, James M. Madden
& Harry Ziegler

THE History PRESS

Published by The History Press
Charleston, SC 29403
www.historypress.net



First published 2014

Manufactured in the United States

ISBN 978.1.62619.357.4

Library of Congress Cataloging-in-Publication Data

Bilby, Joseph G.
350 years of New Jersey history : from Stuyvesant to Sandy / Joseph G. Bilby, James M. Madden and Harry Ziegler.
pages cm
Includes bibliographical references.
ISBN 978-1-62619-357-4
1. New Jersey--History. 2. New Jersey--Biography. I. Madden, James M. (James Martin), 1964- II. Ziegler, Harry F. III. Title. IV. Title: Three hundred fifty years of New Jersey history.
F137.B55 2013
974.9--dc23
2013048440

# Contents

# Acknowledgements

Telling the 350-year story of New Jersey through year-by-year highlights, including military, social, political, cultural, economic and environmental events, is a daunting task. While there are several timelines of the state available, none is a completely satisfactory framework, and the current work required a thorough review of the available literature. Harold F. Wilson's 1950 *Outline History of New Jersey* gave us a good start, and Marc Mappen and Maxine Lurie's *Encyclopedia of New Jersey* proved invaluable, along with the classic, older, multivolume histories by Francis Bazley Lee and Irving Kull, as well as the diverse works of the prolific John Cunningham. We also mined numerous other sources, well known and otherwise, as a glance at the bibliography will reveal.

A number of individuals also contributed ideas, information, stories and photographs, including Henry Ballone; Captain John Bilby, New Jersey National Guard (NJNG); Margaret Bilby; Katherine Bilby Jenkins; Ed Civinskas; John Crowley; Dan Lane; Ron DaSilva; Captain Jarrett Feldman, NJNG; Carol Fowler; Geoffrey Jenkins; Sue Kaufmann; John Kuhl; Frank and Jeammarie McCree; Robert Rudinski; Amanda and Stephanie Simnor; Captain Vincent Solomeno, NJNG; and Jerry Travers. Our thanks are due to all, and our apologies to anyone we inadvertently missed.

# Introduction

In 2014, we celebrate New Jersey's 350th birthday, recalling the day in 1664 when a force dispatched by James, Duke of York, brother of King Charles II of England, sailed into New Netherland waters and captured the Dutch colony's capital of New Amsterdam without a fight. The king granted New Netherland to James, who in turn handed off the sparsely settled land across the river from New Amsterdam to two of his cronies, initiating a centuries-long saga of labyrinthine New Jersey political history down to the present day.

A more positive, and equally interesting, New Jersey heritage is the state's diversity, as an initial population of English and Dutch settlers, free and enslaved African Americans and Native Americans merged over the centuries with waves of immigrants from Ireland, Germany, Italy, Eastern Europe and, in more recent years, all over the world. All found a home in the Garden State. It is no mere coincidence that the Statue of Liberty and Ellis Island are located in New Jersey waters.

Through hundreds of years of war (the "Jersey Blues" have served in every conflict from King James's War in 1694 to Iraq and Afghanistan) and peace, New Jersey's people have had their ups and downs, transitioning from agricultural to industrial and postindustrial economies; pioneering steamboats, railroads, electric lights, traffic circles and drive-in movies along the way, and recovering from setbacks with a brash boosterism belying the storyline that the state is merely a crossroads, the proverbial barrel tapped at opposite ends by New York and Philadelphia.

The state has always been home to outsized personalities active in political, military, economic, entertainment and social fields, some still widely known, others unfairly forgotten, including Elizabeth Haddon, "Scotch Willie" Maxwell, Joseph Bloomfield, Aaron Burr, Sam "Jersey Jumper" Patch, Sam Colt, William Still, Phil Kearny, Leon Abbett, Alice Paul, Thomas Edison, John Draney, Albert Einstein, Moe Berg, James "Jimmy Buff" Racioppi, Curtis Culin and Bruce Springsteen—not to mention the fictional Tony Soprano, played by native "Jersey guy" James Joseph Gandolfini Jr. You will meet them all in the pages of this book, leading you, we hope, to pursue their stories in detail.

It's been a great 350-year ride, and we invite you to come along and experience it, from then to now—and get ready for the next 350.

Chapter 1

# 1664 to 1700

## 1664

In January, the lightly settled land that became New Jersey was part of the Dutch West India Company colony of New Netherland, governed under Director-General Pieter Stuyvesant, who had conquered the Swedish colony along the South (today's Delaware) River in 1656.

On March 12, King Charles II of England granted his brother James, Duke of York, the Dutch colony of New Netherland. The Dutch surrendered to James's English fleet without a fight when it showed up on the doorstep of the colony's capital, New Amsterdam, on August 28. James's deputy governor of the newly named New York, Richard Nicolls, quickly issued land grants or "patents" to draw English settlers from New England and Long Island to the new lands across the river from Manhattan. Although Nicolls was unaware of the fact, James had already granted New Jersey, also known as *Nova Caesaria*, to two of his supporters: Lord John Berkeley and Sir George Carteret. They, in turn, divided the colony into eastern and western portions, with Carteret owning the east and Berkeley the west. The dividing line was unsurveyed and vague. Neither man would ever visit New Jersey.

New Netherland director-general Stuyvesant, who surrendered his colony to Nicolls, had previously authorized resettlement on what became the New Jersey side of what was then the North (today's Hudson) River after Dutch wars with the Native Americans had driven most of the previous settlers there back to New Amsterdam. The new settlement, called Bergen, established in

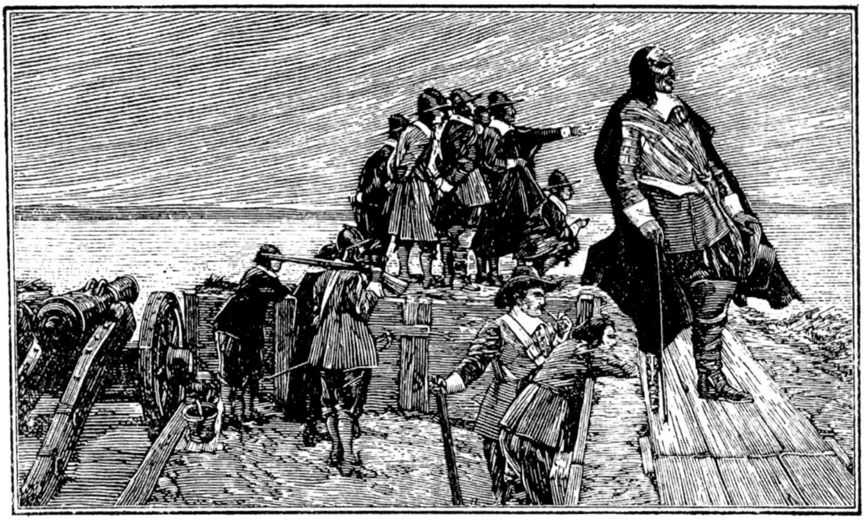

*The Coming of the English* is a nineteenth-century artist's conception of Pieter Stuyvesant observing the impending end of his regime. *James M. Madden.*

1660 on the site of modern Jersey City and considered the first permanent settlement in today's New Jersey, came under English governance. So, for that matter, did Stuyvesant, who, after traveling to the Netherlands to give an accounting of his term in office, returned to New York, where he lived out the rest of his life.

Nicolls's first New Jersey land grant, the "Elizabethtown tract" of over 400,000 acres in the eastern part of the colony, was to Puritans from Connecticut. On October 28, English settlers John Baily, Daniel Denton and Luke Watson exchanged goods with local Native Americans and formally moved into the area.

## 1665

On April 8, Deputy Governor Nicolls granted the "Navesink tract" in today's Monmouth County to Quaker and Baptist settlers from Long Island.

In August, Philip Carteret, a distant cousin of the proprietor, was named the first governor of New Jersey (for all practical purposes actually East New Jersey, where the settlers were at the time). He brought with him a small group of colonists from the Isle of Jersey and landed at Elizabethtown.

The "Concessions and Agreements of the Lords Proprietors" were granted to settlers by Berkeley and Carteret, providing the first New Jersey governing document, along with an assumption that they, and not Nicolls, were the grantees. Among other things, the document granted extra land to settlers holding slaves and guaranteed religious freedom to Protestants. It also set the stage for conflict between Nicolls's grantees and the proprietors regarding property "quitrents" or land-use fees that the proprietors believed to be payable to them.

## 1666

Robert Treat, a Puritan from Connecticut, founded the town of Newark as a theocracy in which only Congregational church members could vote or own property. Although they received the land through Nicolls, Treat and his associates also struck a deal with local Lenape Native Americans, paying them in trade goods for the property, which initially included most of today's Essex County.

## 1667

Hackensack chief Oratam, a key figure who represented Lenape Native American bands in negotiations with the Dutch in New Netherland in the period before the English takeover, died.

## 1668

Philip Carteret called for an assembly to meet in Elizabethtown, with fourteen members from East New Jersey and two from the essentially unsettled area of West New Jersey. The assembly, mostly representing Nicolls's grantees and elected by adult male property owners, met on May 26 for a period of five days and passed militia legislation requiring all men between the ages of sixteen and sixty to muster for "at least four days in the year." There were supposed to be two days of militia training in the spring and two in the fall, with ten days between each training day. Needless to say, such a schedule did not make for a cutting-edge military formation. In order to maintain at least minimal seriousness, the assembly prohibited the sale of liquor to militiamen during drills. Other legislation passed included laws against swearing, drunkenness and fornication, and the death penalty was established for witchcraft.

## 1669

The Township of Woodbridge, located in an area settled by New England Puritans in the early autumn of 1664, was named in honor of Reverend John Woodbridge of Newbury, Massachusetts.

## 1670

When quitrents to proprietors came due on March 25, an organization of settlers was formed in Elizabethtown to resist payment.

New Jersey's population, both east and west, was estimated at one thousand people.

## 1671

Captain James Carteret, son of the proprietor, arrived in Elizabethtown for a visit.

## 1672

Representatives from five of the seven towns then in East New Jersey—Newark, Elizabethtown, Woodbridge, Piscataqua (today's Piscataway) and Bergen (today's Jersey City)—gathered in Elizabethtown on May 14, deposed appointed governor Philip Carteret and elected James Carteret, a "naive young man," as "president of the country." In the end, the king supported the governorship of Philip Carteret, who regained his office.

Quaker founder George Fox traveled to New Jersey to investigate the possibility of establishing settlements there and found it "almost an empty wilderness."

## 1673

War broke out again between the Netherlands and England, and a Dutch fleet recaptured New York and New Jersey from the English, renaming New York City "New Orange." There was no resistance. New Jerseyans of English extraction, including seventy-three of the eighty-four men living in Newark, quickly signed loyalty oaths to the Dutch. The English commander of New York, a man named Manning, was subsequently sentenced by an English court to have "his sword broken over his head" for his lack of combativeness and incompetence. No penalties were imposed on the settlers.

The first Polish immigrant to New Jersey, Olbracht Zaborowski, settled in today's Bergen County. The family name was later changed to Zabriskie.

## 1674

The Treaty of Westminster returned New York and New Jersey to England.

## 1675

Lord Berkeley sold his West New Jersey lands to Quakers Edward Byllynge and John Fenwick. William Penn arbitrated a financial disagreement between Byllynge and Fenwick and became a trustee of West New Jersey.

John Fenwick established a Quaker settlement at Salem in West New Jersey.

New Jersey remained a thinly populated colony. William Edmundsen, a Quaker missionary, landed at the site of today's New Brunswick on the "Rarington River" and traveled overland to the Delaware River without encountering a single settler.

## 1676

On July 1, the "Jerseys" settled their hazy proprietary boundaries by formally dividing into East and West New Jersey on a line drawn diagonally northwest from Little Egg Harbor to a point on the Delaware River slightly north of the Delaware Water Gap. The agreement was signed by Sir George Carteret and the new Quaker proprietors of West New Jersey.

## 1677

A "Concessions and Agreements" document relative to the governance of West New Jersey was drawn up by the Quaker proprietors.

## 1678

On November 10, the *Shield* became the first English vessel to ascend the Delaware River to the site of present-day Burlington, New Jersey. The next morning, the passengers walked ashore on the frozen river. Colonists on the *Shield* and other ships, mostly Quakers, settled at Burlington, Salem and other points along the river, expanding the West New Jersey population, which, until then, had been minimal.

## 1679

Mahlon Stacy and other Quakers established a settlement at the "Falls of the Delaware" River, the site of present-day Trenton.

## 1680

Sir Edmund Andros, royal governor of New York, claimed sovereignty over New Jersey as well and, on April 30, had Philip Carteret beaten and arrested for defying his orders. Andros had Carteret put on trial in May, but the jury failed to convict him of "riot and illegal government," much to Andros's anger, and he was released. Andros was eventually recalled to England, but Carteret died two years later, never having recovered from his injuries.

Proprietor and bungling businessman Edward Byllynge was declared governor of West New Jersey, but he never visited the colony.

The first West New Jersey Assembly met at Burlington.

## 1681

"The Fundamental Agreements of the Freeholders and Inhabitants of the Province of West Jersey," providing for local town governance, was proposed in Burlington on November 25.

Burlington was officially named the West New Jersey capital.

The first house was built on the site of Bordentown by Thomas Farnsworth.

The West New Jersey Assembly authorized the King's Highway, which passed through today's Moorestown, Haddonfield, Woodbury and Swedesboro.

## 1682

On February 1, a group of Quakers, including a number of Scots (although having the same king, Scotland was still considered a separate country from England), bought East New Jersey from George Carteret's widow, thus becoming the new proprietors. Many East New Jerseyans, who had disputed Carteret's proprietorship from the beginning, claimed the sale was illegal, since they had been granted their land by Nicolls and also paid the Lenape for it. The dispute led to generations of political and judicial wrangling and occasional rioting.

Four counties—Bergen, Essex, Middlesex and Monmouth—were created in East New Jersey.

Mark Newbie, a Quaker, opened the first bank in North America in a room of his home near today's city of Camden.

## 1683

A governing document called "The Fundamental Constitutions for the Province of East New Jersey" was adopted. One clause specifically exempted Quakers from militia duty.

West New Jersey proprietor John Fenwick died in Salem.

Miles Forster built a ship in Perth Amboy, thus becoming the first New Jersey boat builder.

## 1684

Disagreements over property and governance issues with no-show West New Jersey governor Byllynge caused a delegation of settlers to travel to England to have their grievances arbitrated.

Lawrie's Road from Perth Amboy to Burlington opened. It was the first road opened to overland transportation in New Jersey.

## 1685

West New Jersey settler Thomas Budd, in his *Good Order Established in Pennsilvania & New Jersey*, a book intended to attract immigrants, wrote that hazards in the colony were "but few in number." He did, however, admit that the marshes were infested by "small Flies, called Musketoes, which are troublesome to such People as are not used to them."

## 1686

The Quakers at Perth Amboy agreed to have a monthly meeting there on "the second 4th day of each Month, and the first to begin the second 4th day of the 9th Month 1686."

The capital of East New Jersey was permanently established at Perth Amboy.

Inian's Ferry, operated by John Inian, was established on the Raritan River at the site of today's New Brunswick.

## 1687

Well-known English court physician and fiscal flim-flam man Dr. Daniel Coxe became governor of West New Jersey by virtue of purchasing a proprietorship from the heirs of Edward Byllynge.

Free African American families from New York secured the Tappan Patent in the Hackensack Valley, becoming the first free black landowners in North America.

## 1688

What became known as "King William's War," the American theater of the European War of the League of Augsberg, began.

Edmund Andros, back in America as governor of the "Dominion of New England," assumed administrative authority over East and West New Jersey though his deputy, Francis Nicholson, who established headquarters in New York.

The first Baptist congregation in New Jersey was founded at Middletown.

Somerset County was created.

## 1689

Following the downfall of Andros and his patron King James, who was replaced by King William and Queen Mary in the "Glorious Revolution" in England, Daniel Coxe resumed his absentee governorship. Like his predecessor, Edward Byllynge, Coxe never visited the colony but was very active in promoting his business interests there.

## 1690

The combined population of East and West New Jersey was eight thousand people.

## 1691

On February 23, "bound servant" Thomas Lutherland was hanged in Salem County for the offenses of robbery and murder.

## 1692

Andrew Hamilton was appointed governor of both East and West New Jersey.

The first post office in New Jersey was established at Perth Amboy. Governor Hamilton was also appointed deputy postmaster general of the American colonies.

Cape May County was created.

## 1693

The second post office in New Jersey was established at Burlington.

## 1694

Burlington and Salem Counties were created.

New Jersey volunteer soldiers were stationed at Albany during King William's War.

## 1695

The first sawmill was built in Newark.

## 1696

A male slave named Jeremy was hanged for murder in Monmouth County.

## 1697

A royal proclamation was issued accusing the English proprietary colonies, including the "Jerseys," of negligence in enforcing the Navigation Acts by allowing the smuggling of goods to and from the colonies in non-English ships.

The West Jersey Assembly authorized the Salem–Cape May highway.

King William's War ended with the Treaty of Ryswick.

## 1698

A West New Jersey promotional pamphleteer wrote "to inform all (but especially the poor) what ample and happy livelihoods people may gain in those parts, whereby they may subsist very well without either begging or stealing."

The East New Jersey Assembly declared that no "free man shall be compelled, enforced, pressed or arrayed" to leave his township for military service save to repel an invasion or by special act of the General Assembly.

The first leather tannery was established in Newark.

## 1699

Captain William Kidd, whose wife was from Monmouth County, dropped anchor in Raritan Bay and sent exploratory parties to New York to see if some political strings could be pulled to drop charges of piracy filed against him. His effort failed, and he was captured later that year in Boston, taken to England, tried for piracy and executed. Legends abound that Kidd buried treasure somewhere along the Raritan Bay coastline, a scenario that is unlikely, to say the least.

## 1700

The year 1700 is the date generally given for the founding of the unique community of Gouldtown, located on the Cohansey River, by Benjamin

Gould. Gould was the son of West New Jersey proprietor John Fenwick's granddaughter, who, to Fenwick's horror, married a free African American man. The community became a multiracial one with white, black and Native American mixed families and has long endured.

New Jersey's population reached ten thousand people.

Lewis Morris, Tinton Falls iron forge owner and slave master, complained that there were too many religious sects and nonbelievers in Piscataway, Middletown, Shrewsbury and Freehold; that there was far too much drinking and carousing on the Sabbath; and that a lack of schools was responsible for the general ignorance of East New Jersey's youth.

## Chapter 2

# 1701 to 1750

## 1701

Quaker Elizabeth Haddon arrived in West New Jersey to manage her father's five hundred acres. She succeeded, married Quaker missionary John Estaugh, became a local herbalist and is considered the founder of Haddonfield.

Arthur Simpson's ferry from Amboy to Navesink opened for business.

## 1702

On March 8, Queen Anne ascended to the throne of England, Scotland and Ireland.

East and West New Jersey were unified as New Jersey, and the proprietors gave up governance, although not all property rights. The colony was governed from New York under Royal Governor Edward Hyde, Lord Cornbury. Cornbury, who was also governor of New York, was a cousin of Queen Anne.

Queen Anne's War, the American theater of the War of the Spanish Succession, began.

In June, a party from a French privateer sailing off Sandy Hook landed at "the Neversinks" on Raritan Bay and plundered several homes before withdrawing.

# 1703

Presbyterian minister Gilbert Tennent, a leading revivalist during the Great Awakening of the 1740s and founding member of the Presbytery of New Brunswick, was born in Ireland on February 5.

In November, Lord Cornbury asked the New Jersey Assembly for "a revenue," or salary. When the legislative body did not come up with a figure, he dismissed it.

# 1704

The New Jersey Assembly reconvened in May, reconsidered Lord Cornbury's request and agreed to pay him £1,000 a year. Cornbury responded that the sum was "not suitable" and dismissed the assembly once again.

The governor refused to seat three Quakers who had been elected to the assembly and, by this bit of political chicanery, was able, through his allies, to gain control of the body by one vote. The assembly then voted to give him a "suitable" salary of £2,000 a year, plus other income and perks.

The assembly passed a law providing for a six-shilling fine for public drunkenness or "breaking the Lord's Day."

A supreme court for the Royal Province of New Jersey was established.

# 1705

The board of trade in England ordered Lord Cornbury to seat the three Quakers he had previously ignored, and he did but then dismissed the entire assembly once again. He and his "ring" of associates then confiscated and sold proprietary lands for their own personal profit.

Essex County established roads to connect the county's growing web of towns. One, Crane Road, still exists as Newark's West Market Street. Another, First Road, is Main Street in Orange.

## 1706

"Huddy's Line," a biweekly freight-hauling service between Perth Amboy and Burlington via Lawrie's Road, was established.

Scotland and England agreed to a treaty of unification as "Great Britain."

## 1707

On May 1, the treaty of unification between Scotland and England became effective, making New Jersey a royal colony of Great Britain.

The assemblies of both New York and New Jersey reconvened and petitioned Queen Anne to remove Lord Cornbury from office.

## 1708

Lord Cornbury's rule came to an end as Queen Anne dismissed him as governor. Jailed in New York, he eventually returned to Great Britain. It has long been asserted that Cornbury was a transvestite, although recent scholarship disputes that.

Queen Anne died on August 1, leaving no surviving children, and was succeeded by King George I, from Hanover, Germany, her closest living Protestant relative, as provided in the "Act of Settlement" of 1701, which prohibited Catholics, even though nominally in the line of succession, from ascending to the throne.

## 1709

New Jersey raised £3,000 to support military operations on land and recruited two hundred volunteers to aid a British fleet in an invasion of Canada. In the event, the fleet never arrived.

## 1710

Robert Hunter, a politically connected lawyer and army officer, arrived in New York to take up his position as royal governor of New York and New Jersey. He brought several thousand Palatinate German refugees to the colonies, and most of them ended up settling in New York and northwestern New Jersey. Hunter raised an additional £5,000 to support the ongoing war and recruited another two hundred volunteers, who were ordered to march to Albany as part of a new campaign to capture Montreal. This operation, known as the "Glorious Enterprise," never got off the ground.

## 1711

Governor Hunter attempted to purge the council, the appointed upper legislative house in New Jersey, of men he believed were blocking his agenda. His political allies in London, however, had lost influence, and he was unable to accomplish his aim.

## 1712

Britain and France declared an armistice, or halt in hostilities, while negotiating a peace treaty.

## 1713

Queen Anne's war formally ended with the Treaty of Utrecht.

## 1714

William Trent bought eight hundred acres of land from Mahlon Stacy Jr. and replaced the log mill at "The Falls" with a sturdier structure, establishing "Trent's Town" on the Delaware.

Hunterdon County was created and named for Governor Hunter. The county included modern Hunterdon, Warren, Sussex, Morris and part of Mercer Counties.

## 1715

Although the Native American population of New Jersey had crashed late in the previous century as many Indians died from introduced European diseases and others left the state to move west, a few Navesink Lenape were still reported to be hunting game and trapping fur-bearing animals to sell to white settlers in Monmouth County.

Quaker John Hepburn authored the first publication advocating the abolition of slavery in New Jersey.

## 1716

A reward was offered by David Lyell, of Amboy and New York, for a runaway slave described as "an Indian man" named Nim, who was apparently looking for a ship to sign on as a crewman in New York.

In an attempt to upgrade the dismal condition of the colony's roads, the New Jersey Assembly passed a law calling for local road overseers to call out inhabitants to repair public roads. Those who did not respond or send a substitute laborer in their place were subject to a daily fine of four shillings, six pence.

## 1717

A male slave named John Hunt was hanged for murder in Salem County.

## 1718

William Penn, founder of Pennsylvania and, along with other Quakers, involved in the West New Jersey proprietorship, died penniless in England on July 30

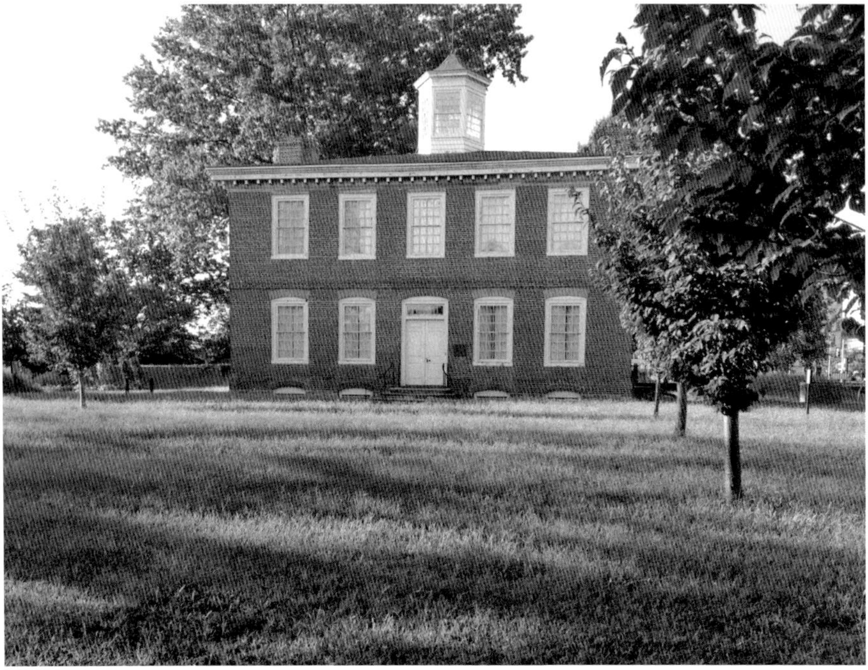

Modern view of the William Trent house. *Geoffrey Jenkins.*

## 1719

John Reading Jr., Joseph Kirkbride and James Alexander surveyed the disputed boundary line between New Jersey and New York.

A special tax to support the poor was initiated in Newark.

The assembly passed a law requiring persons under the age of twenty-one to have their parents' or guardians' written consent to marry.

A large vein of copper ore was discovered at the western edge of the Hackensack Meadows, in today's North Arlington. As the Schuyler family mine, it became very productive for many years, although always subject to flooding.

The William Trent house was built in Trent's Town. Restored in 1934, it still stands.

## 1720

Crusading Quaker preacher and early abolitionist John Woolman was born at Ancocas (today's Rancocas) on October 19.

## 1721

William Trent formally established Trenton.

## 1722

Samuel Dennis Jr. of Shrewsbury advertised for the return of a runaway servant, one "James M'Curdy," who "speaks English and Irish" and "can read and write." A gold coin was promised to whoever retrieved James for Mr. Dennis.

## 1723

Edward Hyde, Lord Cornbury, once royal governor of New York and New Jersey, died in England on March 31. Upon hearing of his death, New Jersey ironmaster Lewis Morris characterized the late royal governor as a "wretch" who had "no regard for honor or virtue."

William Livingston, who would become the first New Jersey governor under the state constitution of 1776, was born in New York.

## 1724

David Drury was hanged in Gloucester County for horse theft.

Inian's Ferry was renamed New Brunswick in honor of the German House of Brunswick of King George I of Great Britain.

## 1725

Jeremiah Basse, who had served as proprietary governor of both East and West New Jersey from 1698 to 1699 as the whole proprietary governing structure began to crumble, died.

## 1726

A census conducted by Royal Governor William Burnet of New York and New Jersey revealed that New Jersey had a population of thirty-six thousand, 92 percent of whom were white and 8 percent of whom were black.

Indentured servant "Sarah Parker or Sartin" ran away from Dr. John Browne with "one Richard Sartin who pretends he is her husband but is not." The person who returned Sarah was promised a reward of forty shillings and expenses.

William Trent's son James began a ferry service from Trenton to Philadelphia.

## 1727

King George I died and was succeeded by his son, who became King George II.

Abigail Sharp sued Abraham Shotwell for allegedly calling her "an old witch" and saying he saw her "flying all night," in addition to appearing atop his house as a cat and bewitching his horse, which subsequently died.

## 1728

Governor Burnet, who lived in New York City and spent as little time in New Jersey as possible, left office and was replaced as governor by John Montgomerie. Montgomerie, a sycophant of King George II, apparently had limited intelligence and a drinking problem to boot.

## 1729

Governor Montgomerie complained to the board of trade in London that the New Jersey Assembly was "unadvisable and ungovernable." At the heart of his problem was the assembly's agitation for a separate governor for the colony.

## 1730

After resisting for over a year, Governor Montgomerie finally passed on the New Jersey Assembly's request for a separate governor to the board of trade.

A witchcraft trial was allegedly held in Burlington, in which the guilt of two people accused of making sheep dance and hogs sing psalms was determined by tossing them into a river to see if they floated or sank. There is no evidence for this story aside from an article in the *Pennsylvania Gazette*, and modern scholars think it was a hoax perpetrated by the paper's publisher, Benjamin Franklin.

## 1731

Governor Montgomerie died of a stroke in New York. A historian has assessed him as "one of the weakest of New Jersey's colonial governors."

## 1732

The first "stage wagon" route in New Jersey was established between Perth Amboy and Burlington. The stagecoach vehicle as we know it was not developed until 1772.

## 1733

William Maxwell was born near Newtonsteward, County Tyrone, Ireland, and emigrated from there with his family to Morris County (in today's

Warren County), New Jersey, in 1747. Maxwell served in the French and Indian War as a junior officer in the New Jersey Provincial Regiment and in the Continental army during the Revolution, when he was known as "Scotch Willie." He rose to the rank of general and commanded the New Jersey Brigade in the Continental army for much of the war. The Jersey general demonstrated considerable tactical ability during the conflict and served in the New Jersey legislature in the postwar era.

## 1734

The legendary Tom Quick, "Indian slayer," was born in New Milford, Sussex County. Quick allegedly killed one hundred Native Americans as revenge for the death of his father, who died in a French and Indian War raid. Although it appears Quick was a real person, there is no historical provenance for the vengeance story, and it must be considered folklore.

An alleged slave rebellion conspiracy was discovered in Somerville, the first such in New Jersey.

## 1735

Thirty-six-year-old indentured servant Martha Brown, characterized as "lusty and well set," ran away from David Heldreth of Shrewsbury. Martha was further described as having "one tooth out and great ringworms on her breast and arms." A reward of twenty shillings and payment of "reasonable charges" was promised for her return.

According to one origin story, the Jersey Devil was born to Mother Leeds in Leeds Point, on the eastern edge of the Pine Barrens. In the immediate aftermath of his birth, the normal-looking baby grew batwings and cloven hooves, among other grotesque features, then flew up the chimney and off into the Pine Woods, where he remains resident to the present day.

## 1736

Governor Montgomerie's successor, William Cosby, generally accounted as a morally dubious character whose primary purpose during his years in office was accumulating a personal fortune, died of tuberculosis in New York.

## 1737

Thomas Paine was born on January 29 in Thetford, England. Paine would write his inspirational pamphlet *The American Crisis* while retreating with George Washington's army across New Jersey in November and December 1776.

## 1738

Lewis Morris of Monmouth County was appointed the first royal governor of the unified colony of New Jersey.

New Jersey's population was assessed at forty-seven thousand, of which 46.9 percent was female.

## 1739

In Newark's first public execution, John Barnes, who also went by several aliases, was hanged on November 17 for burglarizing Thomas Baily's house three times. Apparently not the brightest eighteenth-century New Jersey criminal, Barnes was repentant on the gallows, stating that "all people will take warning by me."

Morris County was created from Hunterdon County and named for then governor Lewis Morris.

The War of Jenkins' Ear began as a conflict between Great Britain and Spain over naval and trading issues, ostensibly when British sea captain Robert Jenkins had his ear sliced off by a Spanish sailor's cutlass in an incident off the coast of South America.

A weekly mail route was established between New York and Philadelphia.

German immigrant Caspar Wistar established New Jersey's first glass factory on Alloway Creek in Salem County. The settlement gained the name Wistarburgh.

A law reminded New Jerseyans that taverns existed to accommodate travelers and strangers and "not for the encouragement of gaming, tippling, drunkenness and other vice so much of late practiced at such places."

# 1740

New Jersey's initial response to hostilities with Spain was to commission privateers sailing out of Perth Amboy to prey on Spanish shipping, but in late 1740, the British government enlisted volunteers from the militia of several colonies, among them New Jersey, and organized these troops into "provincial" units that joined a British army in Jamaica under Admiral Edward Vernon. The New Jersey Assembly appropriated £2,000 to support the expedition, and an unspecified number of Jerseymen boarded ships at Perth Amboy to sail to the Caribbean.

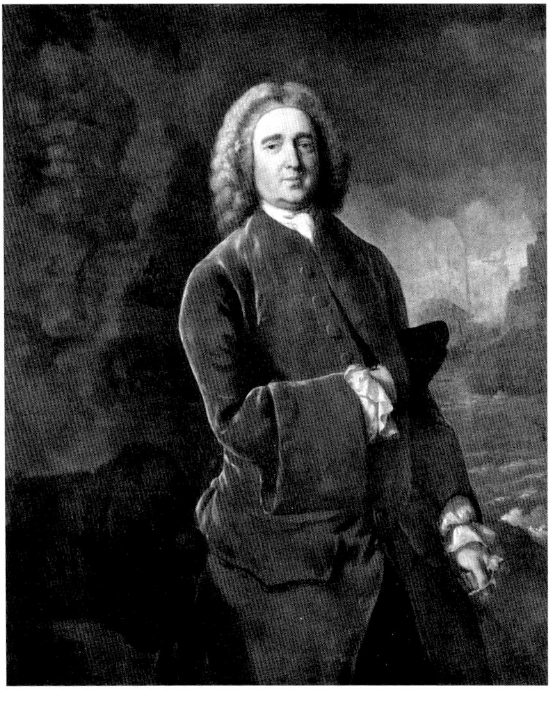

Admiral Edward Vernon led a disastrous attempt to capture Cartagena in 1741. Most of the New Jersey soldiers in his army died as combat casualties or of disease. *Wickimedia Commons.*

Revivalist evangelist George Whitefield preached in Newark at Reverend Aaron Burr's Presbyterian church in November, apparently effectively, as he recalled, "The word fell like a hammer and like fire! What a weeping was there!" The experience of terrifying people so exhausted the preacher that he took to his bed early.

## 1741

Admiral Vernon attacked Cartagena in New Grenada (modern Columbia) at the head of 186 ships and twenty-seven thousand men, the largest amphibious invasion in history until the Normandy landing of 1944, but the expedition ended in disaster. Not only did the British fail to make headway against strong Spanish defenses and an able commander, but also much of Vernon's army, apparently including most of the New Jerseyans enlisted in his ranks, died as combat casualties or of yellow fever.

Rebellious slaves burned seven barns in Hackensack. The alleged perpetrators were subsequently burned alive as punishment.

## 1742

The first blast furnace in New Jersey was established at Ringwood and used to smelt iron ore mined in the Ramapo Mountains.

## 1743

Michael McDonnell was hanged for robbery and murder in Gloucester County.

## 1744

The War of Jenkins' Ear merged with the dynastic struggle in Europe known as the War of the Austrian Succession. France allied itself with Spain and declared war on Great Britain. Fighting began in Nova Scotia as the conflict became known in America as King George's War.

## 1745

A provincial census reported New Jersey's population as 61,383, of whom 4,600 were slaves.

John Dickinson and Gilbert Tennent formed a new Presbyterian Synod for New Jersey.

The New Jersey Assembly appropriated £2,000 to help fund a force that successfully captured the French fortress of Louisburg on Cape Breton Island.

The first in a series of "land riots," ignited by property disputes between settlers and East New Jersey proprietors, began.

The largest lawsuit filed in colonial America was brought by the settlers of Elizabethtown against the East New Jersey proprietors regarding property ownership.

Soldiers were recruited in New Jersey for a provincial regiment. "Freemen and well affected Indians" who enlisted were promised "relief from small debts and pardon from minor crimes." Indentured servants and even slaves could join up without their masters' permission, suggesting a racially integrated organization. Each volunteer received a £6 bounty and was promised "all bounties, plunder and advantages" of regular British army soldiers. The regiment sailed from Newark and Perth Amboy up the Hudson River to Albany under the command of Colonel Peter Schuyler, a wealthy and prominent New Jerseyan whose family owned the copper mine near Newark.

## 1746

Complaints of lack of food, clothing, pay and even weapons from the regiment stationed at Albany made their way back to New Jersey. One private wrote in November that the soldiers were issued "stinking beef," their muskets were "so rusted and rotten so as not to be the value of old iron" and that cutlasses or short swords issued "would bend and stand bent like lead." He blamed contractors into whose hands, for a 5 percent commission, the assembly had placed supply services.

The College of New Jersey, today's Princeton University, was chartered on October 22.

## 1747

The College of New Jersey opened in Elizabethtown but then moved to Newark.

The assembly refused to appropriate more money for its soldiers, and so, in addition to their other miseries, they were not paid. In April, they mutinied, threatening to desert and take whatever public property they could, including weapons, with them. Colonel Schuyler sympathized with his men and, instead of suppressing the mutiny with force, paid them out of his own pocket.

## 1748

The College of New Jersey graduated its first class in Newark.

King George's War ended, and surly New Jersey soldiers returned from Albany, never having seen a shot fired in anger but having suffered more than their share of abuse.

Governor Jonathan Belcher declared New Jersey "the best country I have seen for people who have to live by the sweat of their brows." Needless to say, this did not include him.

Cumberland County was separated from Salem County and named for the Duke of Cumberland.

## 1749

Swedish botanist Peter Kalm visited the Swedish population of southwestern New Jersey, descendants of the old New Sweden colony conquered by the Dutch under Pieter Stuyvesant before their own loss of New Netherland. Kalm interviewed the Swedes and made copious notes, which were later published along with his other observations under the title *Travels in North America*.

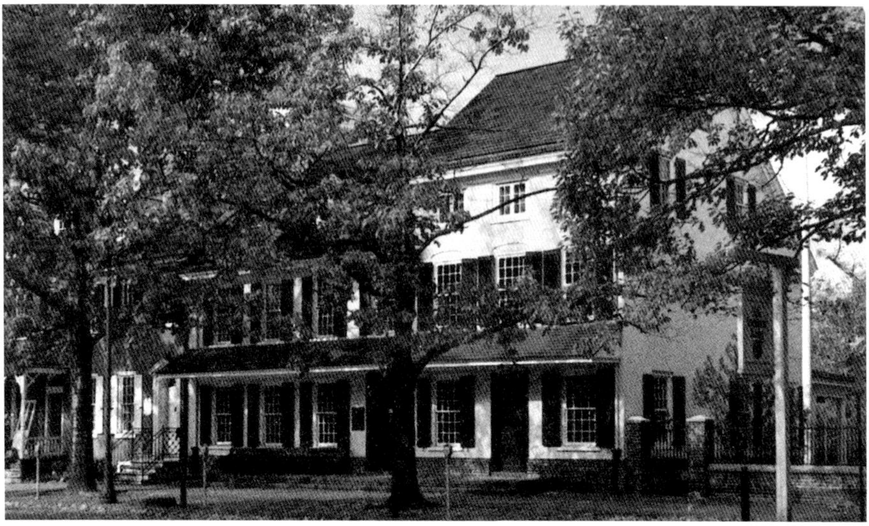

The Indian King Tavern in Haddonfield opened in 1750. The New Jersey legislature met there during the Revolution. *Joseph G. Bilby.*

Middle Forge was established on the Rockaway River in Morris County at the current site of Picatinny Arsenal.

## 1750

The Indian King Tavern in Haddonfield was opened. It served as a meeting place for the New Jersey legislature in 1777 and still stands today.

Dr. Thomas Cadwallader donated money to form the Trenton Library Company, the first public library in New Jersey.

Great Britain, worried about colonial industrial competition, issued an act prohibiting the further construction of slitting or rolling mills. The act was ignored by New Jersey's iron producers.

Chapter 3

# 1751 to 1800

## 1751

A permanent printing press was established at Woodbridge by James Parker.

## 1752

Anti-proprietor quitrent riots occurred in Perth Amboy.

Theater was introduced to New Jersey by a traveling group of British actors known as the "American Company of Comedians," who performed Shakespeare's plays in Perth Amboy.

New Jersey had three post offices, in Perth Amboy, Trenton and Burlington.

## 1753

On October 18, Joseph Bloomfield, future Revolutionary War officer, attorney, politician and governor, was born in Woodbridge. Bloomfield, more than any other politician in the state, was responsible for the eventual passage of a gradual abolition act to end slavery.

The first steam engine in use in America was smuggled out of Great Britain by Josiah Hornblower and used to pump out a flooded shaft at the Schuyler copper mine in Arlington.

Sussex County was created. It included all of present-day Sussex and Warren and was named for an English county.

## 1754

Mary Ludwig Hays, who gained fame as "Molly Pitcher" at the June 28, 1778 Battle of Monmouth Court House, was born, probably in Pennsylvania, although a birthplace near Trenton has also been claimed.

A frontier encounter between George Washington's Virginia soldiers and French troops began what came to be known as the French and Indian War.

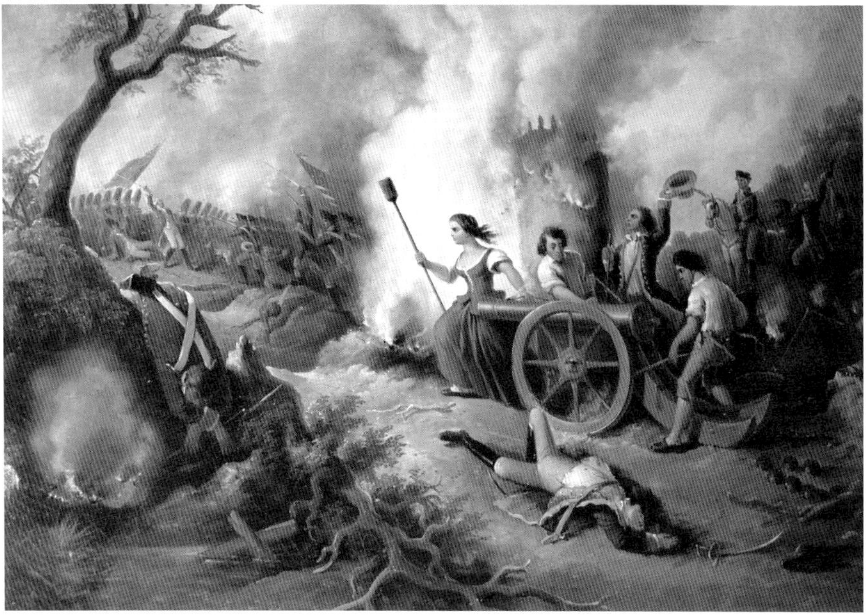

Molly Pitcher, as she was portrayed in a nineteenth-century painting. *Monmouth Battlefield State Park.*

## 1755

At the request of Governor Belcher, the assembly appropriated money to raise a regiment of five hundred men to fight the French. Each recruit was authorized "one good sheepswool blanket, a good lapel coat of coarse cloth, a felt hat, two check shirts, two pair of Osnaberg [muslin] trousers, a pair of shoes and a pair of stockings…a good firelock, a good cutlass sword or bayonet, a cartouche box and a hatchet." Once its ranks were filled, the New Jersey regiment left for Albany.

In November, Governor Belcher ordered militiamen to duty on the Sussex County frontier, then threatened by Indians. An expedition into Pennsylvania failed to intercept the raiders.

## 1756

A January conference was held at Crosswicks between the few remaining resident New Jersey Lenape Native Americans and Governor Belcher. Anxious not to be identified with some of their trans–Delaware River kinsmen who were siding with the French, the New Jersey Indians agreed with the governor's proposals that they relinquish any existing land claims in the colony. In exchange, they were given the opportunity to resettle at a reservation to be established in Burlington County.

Aaron Burr, a future vice president of the United States who would gain historical infamy when he mortally wounded Alexander Hamilton in a duel at Weehawken, was born in Newark on February 6.

In April, Indian raiders, some of them, no doubt, descendants of Lenape refugees from New Jersey, attacked Paulins Kill, and the sixty families living there fled to Amwell.

In June, the colony recruited a full-time "Frontier Guard" unit to be paid two shillings a day per man to occupy blockhouses and patrol along the Delaware River in northwest New Jersey. The Frontier Guards were to supply their own clothing, equipment and weapons, including a "good and sufficient musket."

In August, the French commander in Canada, Major General Louis-Joseph de Montcalm, captured the Oswego forts on Lake Ontario. New Jerseyans serving there, including Colonel Schuyler, became prisoners of war.

# 1757

A call for five hundred volunteers to replace the losses sustained by the New Jersey regiment already in the field was issued. Colonel John Parker replaced Schuyler, now a prisoner in Montreal, in command of the unit. The rebuilt regiment camped at Fort William Henry at Lake George.

On July 21, Fort William Henry commander Lieutenant Colonel George Monro ordered Colonel Parker to take a 350-man force of New Jersey and New York troops up Lake George to determine the location of the French army advancing south. Parker was ambushed at Sabbath Day Point by French soldiers and Indians who opened fire from shore, then encircled his men with canoes. The provincials panicked, losing 160 men killed or drowned and many of the remainder captured, while the enemy lost 1 man wounded.

On August 8, Fort William Henry surrendered to the French, along with the remaining Jerseymen, many of whom were kidnapped by Canadian Indians in the post-surrender massacre made famous in the book and subsequent films titled *Last of the Mohicans*.

Esther Edwards Burr—daughter of famed Great Awakening revival minister Jonathan Edwards; wife of Reverend Aaron Burr, president of the College of New Jersey; mother of future vice president Aaron Burr; and proto-feminist—wrote to her friend Sarah Prince, "I have had a smart combat with Mr. Ewing about our sex. He is a man of good parts and learning but has men thoughts of women." By the time she was done with him, Esther reported, "He blushed and seemed confused."

Royal Governor Jonathan Belcher died on August 31 while attending commencement exercises at the College of New Jersey.

Aaron Burr Sr., founder and president of the College of New Jersey and husband of Esther Edwards Burr, died on September 24.

# 1758

On March 22, Jonathan Edwards, famed preacher best known for the sermon in which he advised parishioners that "God holds you over the pit of hell like a loathsome spider," died at the College of New Jersey in Princeton following a smallpox inoculation. Edwards had replaced Aaron Burr Sr. as college president.

More New Jersey recruits were enlisted to replace those lost at Fort William Henry, and high volunteer bounties were offered to avoid a draft from the militia. The men of the revived regiment left for Albany under the command of Colonel John Johnson in May. Although some cite earlier anecdotal sources, these soldiers were the first Jerseymen officially documented as being uniformed as "Jersey Blues," a nickname that would stick to New Jersey soldiers ever after. They were dressed in "Uniform blue, faced with red, grey stockings and Buckskin Breeches."

On June 14, Francis Bernard arrived in New Jersey to assume the duties of royal governor of the colony.

The "Blues" met with yet another disaster in July 1758, when a British army under General James Abercrombie bungled an attempt to capture Fort Carillon (later Ticonderoga) on Lake Champlain. Abercrombie's army of sixteen thousand men, including the New Jerseyans, vastly outnumbered the French under General Montcalm, but a series of botched frontal assaults on a French defensive line proved disastrous. The Jerseymen did not participate in the worst of the attacks but still lost Lieutenant Colonel Thomas Shaw of Burlington, who, as a captain, had survived the Fort William Henry debacle, along with ten other men killed and forty-four wounded.

In October, Pennsylvania and New Jersey attempted to settle remaining Indian land claims against their states in the Treaty of Easton. New Jersey Lenape Indians who had moved west of the Delaware River from northern New Jersey in previous years were given a cash settlement.

Five permanent barracks to house British soldiers were built in various New Jersey towns, including Perth Amboy and Trenton. The Trenton "Old Barracks," now a museum, is the only one to survive to the present day.

Many of the southern New Jersey Lenape, who gave up their claims at Crosswicks in 1756, elected to move to the Brotherton Reservation in Burlington County. Others continued to live in small, out-of-the-way communities, often composed of mixed race people.

James Parker published the *New American Magazine* at his press in Woodbridge. It was the first periodical written, edited and printed in New Jersey.

## 1759

Although some say it was in use as a popular nickname as early as 1747, the first documented use of the term "Jersey Blues" to describe New Jersey soldiers was used in a letter.

Approximately three hundred Christian Lenape were still living in New Jersey, perhaps a third of them at the Brotherton Reservation. John Brainerd, a Presbyterian missionary, moved to Brotherton, and Lenape interpreter Stephen Calvin established a school at the reservation.

Traveler Andrew Burnaby reported that New Brunswick had "a number of beauties" and, along with Philadelphia, had "the handsomest women that I saw in America." His impression of Newark was that the only noteworthy object in the "irregular, scattered" town was the Trinity Church spire.

## 1760

The popular election of road overseers and surveyors was established by the assembly.

## 1761

The "Jersey Blues" were assigned to garrison duty at Oswego, now back in British hands.

## 1762

The Seven Stars Tavern in Salem County was allegedly the first drive-in restaurant in New Jersey. Visitors on horseback could be served food and drink from a special window. It should be noted that a similar claim is made for the Stone Tavern in Greenwich, Cumberland County, which supposedly offered such service as early as 1728.

## 1763

The French and Indian War ended and, along with it, the French empire in North America with the signing of the Treaty of Paris.

William Franklin, Benjamin Franklin's illegitimate son, was named royal governor of New Jersey.

Cornelius Low of Raritan Landing advertised for a runaway slave, name not noted, who was "an extremely handy fellow at any common work," was wearing a surplus French army uniform, spoke "very good English and Low Dutch and pretty good High Dutch" and apparently intended to "pass himself off as a freeman" and secure a job as a merchant sailor.

## 1764

Sandy Hook lighthouse, the oldest still-operating lighthouse in the United States, began operation on land purchased by New York City on Sandy Hook peninsula.

Proprietary House, the only still-standing colonial governor's residence in the United States, was completed in Perth Amboy, and William Franklin moved in as the first and last royal governor to occupy it.

## 1765

The Stamp Act passed the British Parliament, and the New Jersey Assembly sent delegates to the Stamp Act Congress, held in protest in New York in October.

Iron entrepreneur and businessman Charles Read bought several thousand acres of Pineland property from Richard Wescoat for £200.

## 1766

William Dunlap was born in Perth Amboy on February 19. Dunlap was the first American professional playwright who made a living off of his writing. His best-known work is *The Life of Major Andre*, which he wrote in 1798.

Charles Read established an iron furnace at Batsto on the property he purchased from Richard Wescoat.

Queen's College (today's Rutgers University) was chartered by "New Side" Dutch Reformed Church clergymen in New Brunswick.

The Medical Society of New Jersey was founded in New Brunswick. It was the first medical society in America.

## 1767

In June, the British Parliament passed the Townshend Acts, which created a tax on goods imported by colonists, such as paper, red and white lead, glass, paints and tea shipped from England. The law proved very unpopular and was one of the causes of the American Revolution.

## 1768

A burglar broke into the Perth Amboy home of New Jersey treasurer Stephen Skinner and made off with the treasury, some £6,750, causing a governmental crisis. The crime was never solved, and some suspected the treasurer himself, who subsequently became a Loyalist leader in the Revolutionary War.

## 1769

An ongoing conflict regarding the border between New York and New Jersey was settled by a royal commission appointed in October. The commissioners established what would become the permanent and final border that runs southeast from the confluence of the Delaware and Neversink Rivers near Port Jervis to the Hudson River.

A boycott of British goods, which began in Massachusetts in response to the Townshend Acts, reached New Jersey.

## 1770

In an Essex County riot protesting the actions of lawyers and creditors, "Liberty Boys" waved banners bearing the words "Liberty and Property," and some set fire to the property of David Ogden, a prominent attorney.

# 1771

Queen's College classes began at the Sign of the Red Lion Tavern at the corner of Albany and Neilson Streets in New Brunswick. The site is now on the Johnson and Johnson Corporation property.

# 1772

William Livingston, who would become a towering figure in early New Jersey history as militia commander and governor, moved to Elizabethtown from his native New York.

The New Jersey Assembly passed a bill requiring a license to practice medicine.

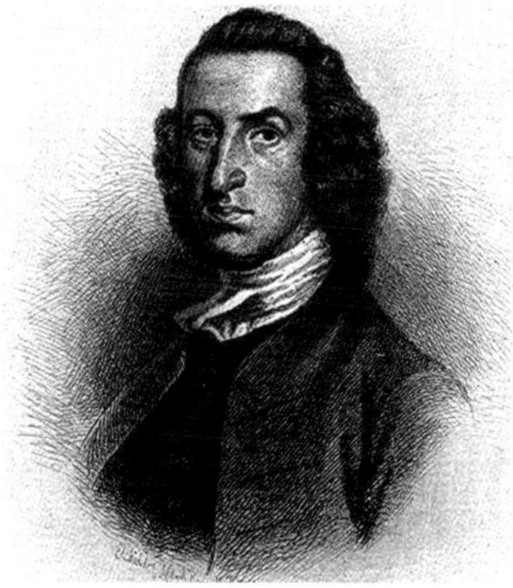

William Livingston. From Lossing, *Pictorial Fieldbook.*

# 1773

Richard Kimball of Morris County imported a twelve-gallon copper still from England to make applejack, also known as "Jersey Lightning."

# 1774

On December 22, a "Tea Party" inspired by the Boston incident of the previous year was held in Greenwich. Tea that had been unloaded from a British ship whose captain was afraid of docking at Philadelphia was burned in the street by "Indians."

The Ford Mansion in Morristown, which served as George Washington's headquarters during the Revolution and is now part of Morristown National Park, was built.

## 1775

New Jersey had two opposing representative legislative bodies: the General Assembly, recognized by Royal Governor William Franklin, and the Provincial Congress, representing those who opposed British control of the colony. The Provincial Congress also created a Committee of Safety, which in turn created militia "Minute Man" companies. As shooting started at Lexington and Concord in Massachusetts in April, tensions rose in New Jersey. In the end, the Provincial Congress won out, and Governor Franklin was arrested in Perth Amboy for continuing to communicate with royal authorities.

In October, the Provincial Congress, at the request of the Continental Congress, voted to raise two eight-company battalions of Continental or regular army soldiers for one-year enlistments. The battalions were sworn into Continental service in December.

## 1776

New Jersey's Provincial Congress passed a resolution to form a government "for regulating the internal police of this Colony." A committee of ten members of the congress was subsequently appointed to draw up a state constitution, which was adopted on July 2. William Livingston was chosen as the first state governor under the new constitution, which was the only one of the original state constitutions granting the right of suffrage to women, providing they were property owners.

The First and Second Battalions, New Jersey Continental Line, engaged in combat with British forces in Canada in June.

In late June, British general William General Howe arrived off Staten Island with a fleet and an army to capture New York, a task he approached in a leisurely manner.

On July 4, former royal governor William Franklin, arrested and detained at his Burlington estate in January, arrived in Connecticut as a prisoner of war. He was exchanged in 1778 and returned to New York to head a Loyalist group that waged war on New Jersey.

In July, Continental army general Hugh Mercer established Fort Delancy at Bergen Neck, in today's Bayonne, to counter the British presence on Staten Island. The fort was later abandoned when the British took control of New York.

In November, after a series of American defeats on Long Island and in New York, a British and Hessian force stormed Fort Washington, across the Hudson River from New Jersey, and captured 2,600 Americans. Morale on the Jersey side of the river, where soldiers watched the disaster unfold from Fort Lee, plummeted, and the Americans began to evacuate supplies inland as British troops began to cross the river. After British soldiers scaled the Palisades, Fort Lee was abandoned, and Washington began his retreat across New Jersey to Pennsylvania.

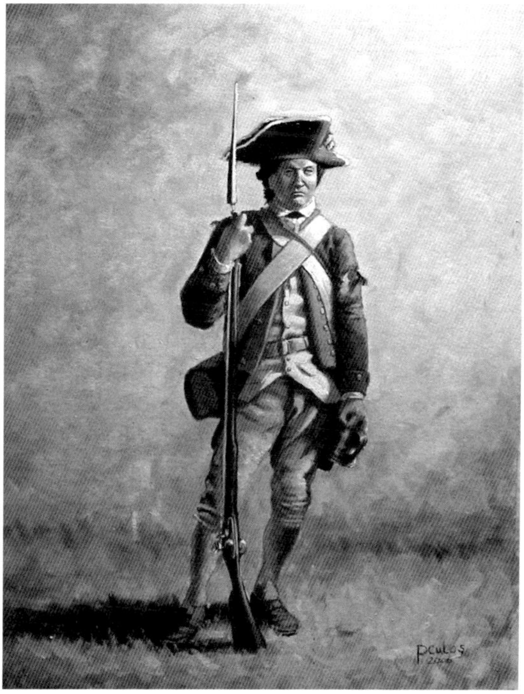


Soldier of the Second New Jersey Continental Battalion, 1778. *Peter Culos.*

American general Charles Lee, a former British officer, was captured while dallying at Basking Ridge.

The Provincial Congress ordered militiamen to suppress Tory demonstrators in Hunterdon County and directed the arrest of others in Monmouth County's Upper Freehold and Shrewsbury Townships, where Loyalist agents were active and somewhat successful in exploiting Quaker ambivalence about the war and translating it into active opposition to the Patriot cause.

On Christmas night, General George Washington led 2,400 men across the Delaware from Pennsylvania in rain, sleet and snow at McKonkey's Ferry, north of Trenton. At 4:00 a.m. the following day, the force marched south in two columns, entering Trenton and routing the Hessian garrison. Washington returned to Pennsylvania but came back to Trenton several days later and prepared to fight a British force advancing from Princeton.

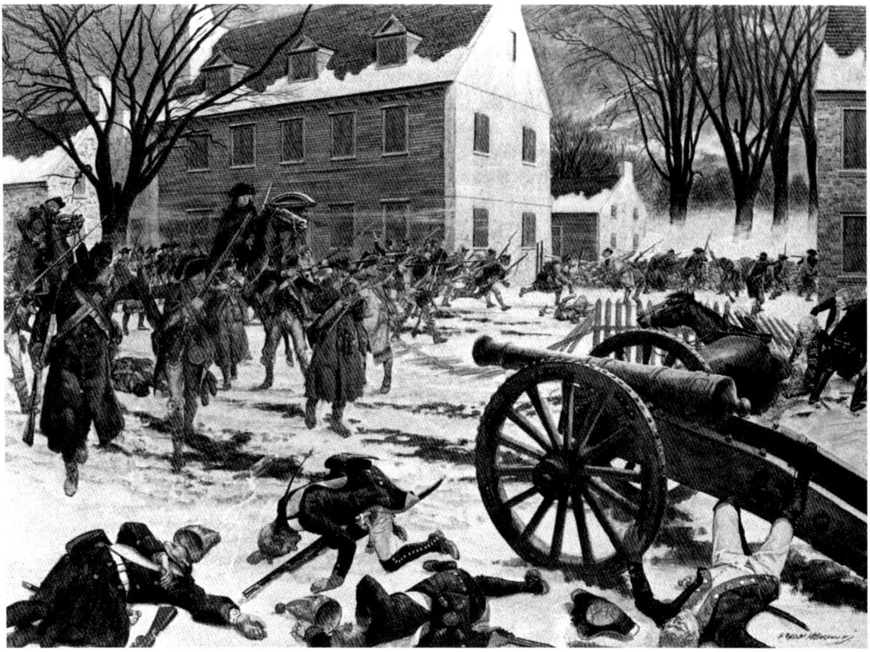

The Battle of Trenton, December 26, 1776. *National Guard Militia Museum of New Jersey (NGMMNJ).*

Colonel Jacob Ford Jr. built the first gunpowder mill in New Jersey in Morristown.

The Philadelphia Quaker yearly meeting banned the ownership of slaves by its members.

## 1777

Following the inconclusive Second Battle of Trenton along Assunpink Creek, General Washington disengaged his army from contact with the British and slipped away during the night of January 2, headed for Princeton. Washington defeated a British force at Princeton on January 3 and quickly moved on to Morristown, where he established a winter camp and rebuilt his army. His actions in those critical days saved the Revolution.

On January 12, Continental army general Hugh Mercer died of the bayonet wounds he received at Princeton. Mercer County was subsequently named in his honor.

In late January, New Jersey mounted militiamen captured a British supply wagon train in Somerset County, in the beginning stages of what came to be known as the Forage War. The intensity of militia activity, supported by William Maxwell's Jersey Continental troops, led General Howe to evacuate British troops from Elizabethtown.

In late February, British lieutenant-colonel Charles Mawhood led a strong British force out of Perth Amboy toward Rahway. "Scotch Willie" Maxwell was happy to accommodate Mawhood's apparent desire for a fight. The British tried to outflank a line of militiamen with a company of grenadiers from the Forty-second Highland Regiment, but Maxwell had deployed more Jerseymen, who remained unseen, in a position outflanking the advance, and at the appropriate moment, they rose and shot the regulars to ribbons.

By spring, the force under George Washington's direct command at Morristown reported 7,363 officers and men "fit for duty and on duty." Arms and ammunition began to arrive in large quantities from France, with nineteen thousand muskets and one thousand barrels of gunpowder imported during the month of March alone.

Washington led his army across New Jersey and into Pennsylvania in an attempt to block a British force advancing under General Howe on Philadelphia. The Americans were defeated at the Battle of Brandywine on September 11.

Following Brandywine and the subsequent fall of Philadelphia, Hessian attackers suffered a disastrous defeat when their October 22 attack on American Fort Mercer, on the New Jersey banks of the Delaware River below Philadelphia, was repulsed. The Hessians suffered four hundred casualties, including their commander, Colonel Carl Von Donop, who was killed in the fight.

In November, New Jersey Militia general Philemon Dickinson led a force of 1,400 militiamen on a massive raid on Staten Island and captured two hundred soldiers of the Loyalist New Jersey Volunteers, most of them recently recruited in Bergen County.

The *New Jersey Gazette*, the state's first newspaper, began publication in Burlington on December 5.

The New Jersey state seal was approved at a legislative meeting held at the Indian King Tavern in Haddonfield.

Hobart's Gap to Morristown. Hannah Ogden Caldwell, wife of American clergyman and Patriot activist Reverend James Caldwell, was killed on June 6 when a British soldier fired into her house in Connecticut Farms (today's Union). American resistance from militia and Continentals gradually stiffened, and Knyphausen's advance slowed when General Maxwell arrived with reinforcements. Maxwell conducted a fighting withdrawal across the Rahway River toward Springfield, and by nightfall on June 7, Knyphausen gave up and withdrew.

Later in the month, Knyphausen made a second incursion into New Jersey in hopes of capturing Hobart's Gap and Morristown. This time he was supported by diversionary forces to the north. The British column moved through Connecticut farms but was halted at Springfield on June 23, and Knyphausen withdrew once more. Springfield was the last significant battle in the north during the Revolution.

The first meeting of the Association for Retaliation, an extra-legal organization created for the sole purpose of harassing known local Loyalists and their suspected sympathizers still residing in Monmouth County by using some of the same violent tactics employed by Tory refugee groups, was held in Freehold. The participants in the meeting drafted a constitution entitled "The Articles of Association for Purposes of Retaliation," a document that clearly exemplifies the principle of an "eye for an eye."

## 1781

In January, the Pennsylvania Line regiments of the Continental army, encamped for the winter at Jockey Hollow near Morristown, mutinied over a lack of supplies, length of service and pay issues. The mutiny ended in a negotiated settlement.

New Jersey soldiers camped at Pompton also mutinied, asking for the same settlement terms as their fellow soldiers of the larger Pennsylvania Line. Instead, they were forced to surrender, and the three sergeants who led the rebellion were executed.

Professed Loyalist and bandit Joe Mulliner was hanged near Pleasant Mills on August 8.

On November 24, Reverend James Caldwell was shot and killed by an American sentry on duty at Elizabethtown. It was believed that the Loyalists had bribed the sentry to commit the act, and he was tried and executed for murder.

A petition to the New Jersey legislature requested that body to pass legislation mandating the gradual abolition of slavery. There was no action on the petition.

## 1782

Toms River was burned by Loyalist raiders, who captured well-known Monmouth County Patriot leader Captain Joshua Huddy. Huddy was subsequently hanged by Loyalists in revenge for the death of one of their own, Philip White, who, after capture, was killed while allegedly trying to escape. The killing of Huddy gave rise to an international incident when George Washington reluctantly picked a British officer, Charles Asgill, to execute in retaliation. Diplomatic intervention ended the crisis and saved Asgill.

## 1783

A majority of the members of the Continental Congress voted to leave Philadelphia and establish a new capital at Trenton, New Jersey. Fortunately or unfortunately, southern congressmen refused to agree and a two-thirds majority, necessary to approve appropriations for the move, was not achieved.

The American War for Independence formally ended with the signing of the Treaty of Paris on September 3.

## 1784

John Stevens, an important New Jersey legislator during the Revolution, bought a large tract of land that would become Hoboken.

## 1785

The Moorestown Friends School was founded by Quakers.

# 1786

The New Jersey legislature granted John Fitch of Trenton the exclusive right of building and operating steamboats on all the waters of New Jersey for a fourteen-year period.

A law was enacted forbidding the further importation of slaves, and one of the provisions made it easier for owners to free their slaves.

# 1787

The Presbyterian Synod of New Jersey called for using "prudent measures to secure the eventual abolition of slavery in America."

The "New Jersey Plan," which was submitted by New Jersey's delegates to the Constitutional Convention, provided the basis for states' equal representation in the United States Senate.

On December 18, New Jersey was the third state to ratify the United States Constitution.

John Fitch demonstrated his steamboat on the Delaware River on August 22.

New York declared that all vessels bound to or from New Jersey ports should pay customs duties to New York. In retaliation, New Jersey taxed the Sandy Hook lighthouse, which was erected on four acres purchased by the City of New York.

# 1788

John Fitch launched a sixty-foot-long steam-powered paddle boat that carried thirty passengers at a time between Burlington and Philadelphia. The thirty-mile trip took three hours and ten minutes.

The Jersey shore was born as a vacation destination as the first vacationers arrived at a boardinghouse in Long Branch.

Governor William Livingston urged the legislature to pass a law providing for the gradual abolition of slavery. The legislators declined to do so.

# 1789

James Fenimore Cooper was born in Burlington on September 15.

On November 20, New Jersey became the first state to ratify the Bill of Rights.

# 1790

Governor William Livingston died in office on July 25.

The first United States census reported New Jersey's population as 184,139, including 11,423 slaves. Bergen County (today's Bergen and Hudson Counties) had 2,300 slaves, the highest percentage of the population of any county, at 19.8 percent.

Trenton was officially named the state capital.

# 1791

On November 4, General Arthur St. Clair's army, including a battalion recruited in New Jersey, met disastrous defeat by Indians under the command of Chief Little Turtle on the Wabash River in Ohio. Scarcely 500 of St. Clair's men escaped uninjured. Over the course of its service, from May through November 1791, 328 officers and men served in the New Jersey battalion. Of these, 34 deserted, 5 died of undisclosed causes, 51 were killed or went missing (presumed dead) and 8 were wounded but escaped.

The Society for Establishing Useful Manufactures (aka Society for the Establishment of Useful Manufactures), or SUM, was chartered. The organization, brainchild of assistant Treasury secretary Tench Coxe and sponsored by Treasury secretary Alexander Hamilton, intended to create a city to promote industry along the stretch of the Passaic River where the falls of the river provided power for mills and factories. The city was named Paterson after New Jersey governor William Paterson.

# 1792

Sara Moore Grimke was born in South Carolina on November 26. Grimke and her younger sister, Angelina Grimke Weld, were raised in a slaveholding family but became abolitionists. The sisters moved to New Jersey and lived in Fort Lee, Belleville, Englewood and, lastly, Perth Amboy, where they were deeply involved in the Raritan Bay Union's coeducational and interracial Eagleswood School in the 1850s.

The federal Militia Act of 1792 cited the obligation of all males within certain age parameters to render military service when called on, and New Jersey passed its own Militia Act in 1792 to comply with the federal legislation. Although the entire able-bodied male population of the state was considered to be the "militia" and therefore subject to service, the state legislation authorized the counties to create companies of light infantry, grenadiers, cavalry and artillery that would "dress themselves in uniform regimentals" as a more active force.

The New Jersey General Assembly met in the still-unfinished statehouse in Trenton. The basic building, with additions and modifications, still stands today, as the second-oldest state capitol building in continuous use.

# 1793

America's first aerial flight occurred on January 9, when Jean François Blanchard piloted his balloon from Philadelphia to Deptford (today's Woodbury). The trip took him forty-six minutes.

Quaker Abigail Goodwin was born on December 1 in Salem. Goodwin became a staunch abolitionist and maintained an important stop on the New Jersey branch of the Underground Railroad. She lived to see the end of slavery before her death on November 2, 1867.

The New Jersey Society for the Abolition of Slavery was founded.

A traveler complaining about the state of New Jersey's roads wrote: "If the surgeons of Princeton object to having the roads mended for fear travelers will have no bones broken, they ought to get their bones broken!"

Connecticut state treasurer Peter Colt came to Paterson to manage the SUM town on the Passaic, replacing Pierre L'Enfant when L'Enfant's grandiose plans for the city ran through investors' money and proved impractical. L'Enfant went on to design the layout of the national capital of Washington, D.C. The Colt family would have a long relationship with Paterson, but the best-remembered member would be the one whose business failed there—Samuel Colt.

## 1794

Governor Richard Howell, who had served as an officer in the Revolution, led the New Jersey militia into Pennsylvania as part of a force called up by President George Washington to help quell the "Whiskey Rebellion," initiated by the refusal of rural western whiskey producers to pay a federal excise tax. The rebellion collapsed without any fighting, and Governor Howell is crediting with writing "Dash to the Mountains, Jersey Blue," a song about the campaign. The term "watermelon army" was coined by the Pennsylvanians to characterize the New Jersey militia, but the origins of the nickname, assumed to be pejorative, are unknown.

Nicholas Roosevelt made the first steam engine fabricated entirely in America in his shop in Belleville.

## 1795

Queen's College closed temporarily due to financial troubles. It reopened in 1807.

A law providing for the gradual abolition of slavery failed to pass the New Jersey legislature by one vote.

## 1796

A library was established in Trenton for the use of the state government.

## 1797

On June 17, Charles Newbold of Chesterfield Township in Burlington County patented an improved plow, with iron moldboard, share and landside cast of iron in one piece at Hanover Furnace. In practice, the device did not work out, as conservative local farmers refused to consider it over the traditional wooden plow, some allegedly maintaining that the iron poisoned the ground, and he ceased manufacturing it.

## 1798

A wooden toll bridge was built over the Hackensack River between Newark and Jersey City.

The farm periodical *Rural Magazine* began publication in Newark.

Governor Howell proposed to raise a regiment when tensions with France spilled over into naval conflict in 1798, but his offer was declined by the federal government.

## 1799

Charles Smith Olden, governor of New Jersey at the outbreak of the Civil War, was born on February 19 into an old and established Quaker family in Stony Brook, near Princeton.

Chester Township, Morris County, was established by the state legislature as the result of a public referendum. The township was created using land from Roxbury and Washington Townships.

## 1800

The federal census reported New Jersey's population as 211,149.

David Naar was born a Sephardic Jew in Saint Thomas, Virgin Islands, on November 10. Narr immigrated with his family to New York and then New Jersey and became deeply involved in New Jersey Democratic Party politics. In 1853, he bought the *Trenton True American* newspaper, which he used as a platform for defending the institution of slavery and later attacking the Lincoln administration during the Civil War at every opportunity, although never advocating a Confederate victory, which made him a "moderate copperhead."

## Chapter 4

# 1801 to 1850

## 1801

Ellis Hughes, owner of the Hotel Atlantic in Cape May, placed a spring advertisement in the *Philadelphia Daily Aurora*, extolling his seaside location and "extensive houseroom, with fish, oysters, crabs and good liquors." The stagecoach from Cooper's Ferry (today's Camden), Hughes noted, left every day for Cape May.

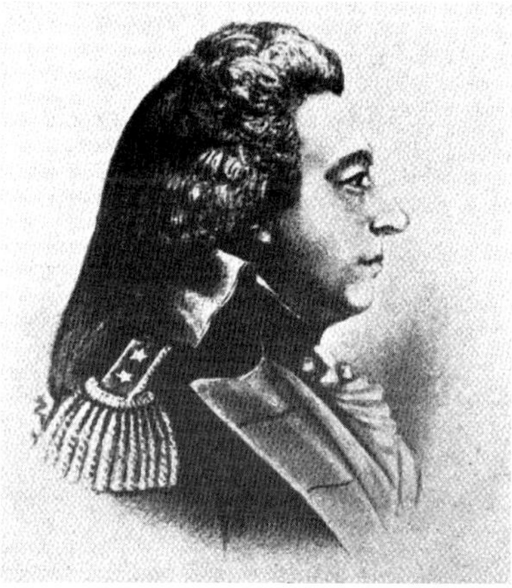

Joseph Bloomfield, Revolutionary War soldier, governor and early abolitionist. *Wickimedia Commons.*

State elections held in September resulted in victory for the Jeffersonian Republicans, and Joseph Bloomfield was elected governor for a one-year term by the legislature. Bloomfield was reelected every year through 1812, save one in which there was no governor. He had a particular interest in the abolition of slavery, and although the governor did not have a great deal of political power under the Constitution of 1776, Bloomfield eventually managed to get a gradual abolition law passed.

# 1802

George Ashbridge, manager of Weymouth Furnace in the Pine Barrens, advertised for "a full set of forgemen to work a new forge, now erected and in complete order" as the bog iron industry began to take off.

The few remaining Lenape Indians at the Brotherton reservation, which had never become self-sufficient as planned, left New Jersey to join the Oneida Indians in New York.

# 1803

Joseph Alexander Adams, a noted engraver who performed work for leading book publishers and newspapers in the early to mid-nineteenth century and also made contributions to electrotyping, was born in New Germantown (today's Tewksbury Township).

Samuel Francis Du Pont was born at Bergen Point on September 27. A navy captain in 1861, Du Pont organized the blockade of the Confederacy and led several successful amphibious operations. After his failed attack on Charleston in 1863, he was relieved of combat duty and spent the rest of the war on administrative service.

# 1804

On February 18, an "Act for the Gradual Abolition of Slavery," promoted by Governor Bloomfield, became law in New Jersey. Enslaved persons born before July 4, 1804, were to remain in servitude, while children born after that date were to be freed at the ages of twenty-one for females and twenty-five for males. New Jersey was the last northern state to end slavery.

On July 11, a longstanding political feud ended when Alexander Hamilton was mortally wounded in a duel with Aaron Burr at Weehawken. Hamilton died the following day in New York City, and Burr subsequently fled the state when indicted for murder by a Bergen County jury. The indictment was later quashed by the New Jersey Supreme Court.

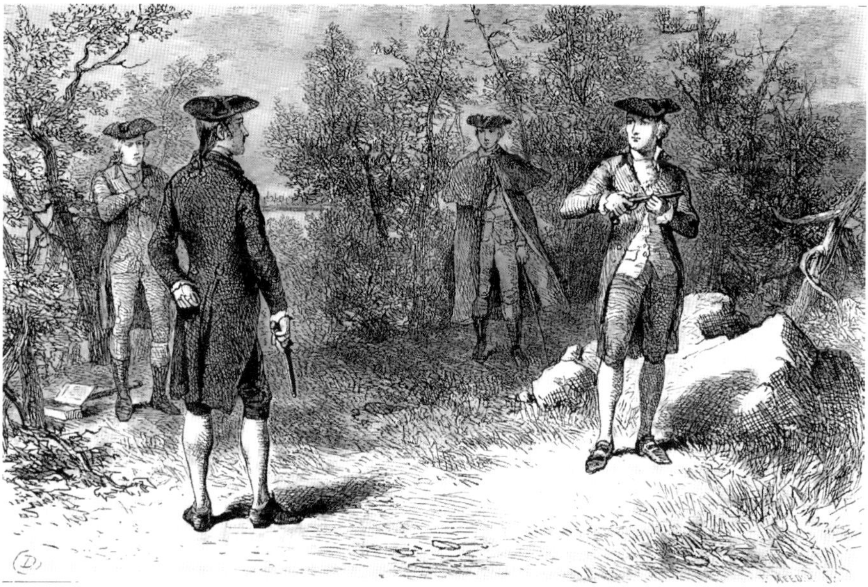

A late nineteenth-century illustration of the Burr-Hamilton duel in Weehawken. From Lamb, *History of the City of New York*.

On September 4, during the First Barbary War, U.S. Navy captain Richard Somers of Egg Harbor was killed along with his volunteer crew when *Intrepid*, a "fire ship" that he was attempting to sail into Tripoli Harbor, exploded prematurely. He was buried on the shore. In 2004, the New Jersey Assembly passed a resolution requesting the return of Somers's remains from Libya. As of the date of this writing, that has not occurred.

## 1805

Lieutenant Zebulon Pike, born in Somerset County in 1779, the son of a New Jersey Continental army officer of the same name, was ordered by General James Wilkinson, governor of the Upper Louisiana Territory, to find the source of the Mississippi River. Pike traveled upriver from Saint Louis into the northern part of the territory on this quest.

## 1806

The first bridge spanning the Delaware at Trenton, a toll bridge owned by the Trenton Delaware Bridge Company, was opened on January 30.

A catalogue issued by Daniel Smith of Burlington, an early fruit tree nursery owner, listed sixty-seven varieties of peach trees.

One-third of all Newark's residents made their living making boots and shoes.

## 1807

Voting rights were amended to include only white male taxpayers, correcting an unintentional oversight by the white males who drew up the Constitution of 1776, which allowed women and free black male property owners to vote. They were now denied the franchise.

## 1808

Nineteen-year-old Allamuchy Quaker Benjamin Lundy visited Wheeling, Virginia, where he saw slaves being herded into "stockyards" for sale. He was so appalled by the sight that he became a lifelong abolitionist and allegedly brought William Lloyd Garrison to the cause.

## 1809

On January 7, Caleb Earle, clerk at Martha Furnace, a Pine Barrens bog iron manufacturing town, noted that "ore teams hauled hay. Blew the furnace out at 8 o'clock p.m. All hands drunk."

Hampered from operating his steamboat *Phoenix* on the Hudson River profitably due to restrictions imposed by Robert Fulton's New York State–granted monopoly, John Stevens of Hoboken sailed the ship down the New Jersey coast and up the Delaware River to Trenton in June, making the *Phoenix* the first steam-powered vessel to operate on the Atlantic Ocean.

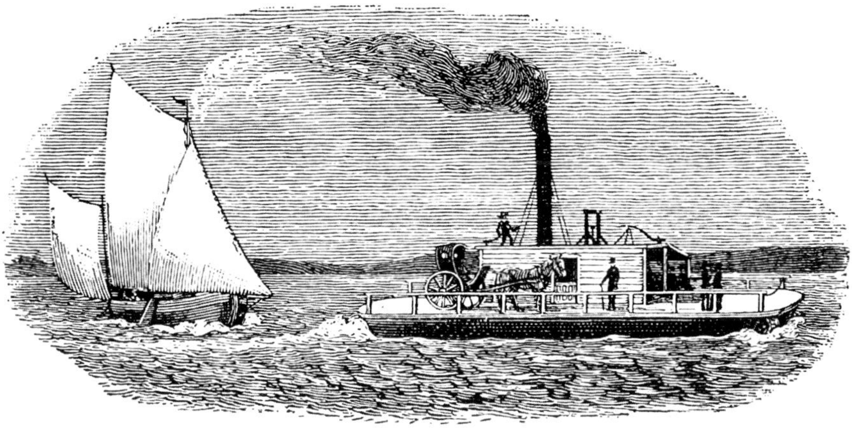

An early steam ferry crossing the Hudson River. *James M. Madden.*

# 1810

The census reported that New Jersey's population was 245,562, a 16.3 percent increase over 1800.

James W. Marshall was born in Hopewell Township on October 8 at the Round Mountain Farm, still known as Marshall's Corner. In 1816, the Marshall family relocated to a house in nearby Lambertville that still stands. James left New Jersey in 1834 and headed west. On January 24, 1848, while building a mill for John Sutter in Coloma, California, he discovered gold, the first find of what would become the California gold rush.

By the end of the year, there were two gunpowder plants in New Jersey, the Decataur mill in Second River (today's Belleville) and the Gentlemen's Powder Mill of Spotswood.

The Merino sheep mania hit New Jersey via New England. The Merino, imported initially from Spain, was thought by many to be the perfect livestock. Within five years, there were twenty-five thousand Merino sheep in New Jersey, half in the southern counties of Burlington, Salem and Gloucester. *Rural Visitor* magazine, published in Burlington, promoted the movement, which went into decline after 1820.

# 1811

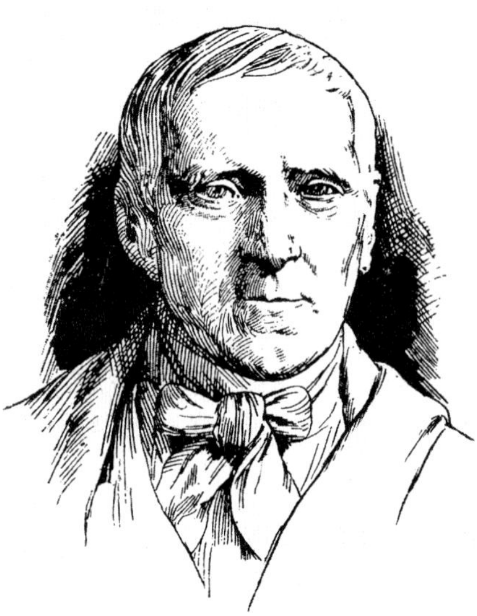

John Stevens applied for a railroad charter between Trenton and New Brunswick in 1811. From Kull, *History of New Jersey*.

On April 1, the Martha Furnace clerk noted, "Finished killing hogs about sunset. Hands kept sober. Cross driving his team. It was said Cross put his wife out of doors and told her to seek 'lodgins.'"

On August 20, the Martha Furnace clerk recorded in his diary, "Peter Cox got very drunk and gone to bed. Mr. Evans made a solemn resolution any person or persons bringing liquor to the works enough to make drunk shall be liable to fine."

On October 11, the first steam ferry, John Stevens's *Juliana*, began to run across the Hudson River between New York and Hoboken.

John Stevens applied for a railroad charter for a line between Trenton and New Brunswick. He was granted the first railroad charter in America in 1815, but the line was not built.

# 1812

On June 18, America declared war on Great Britain.

Steamboat developer Robert Fulton noted the advantageous location of Paulus Hook for commerce and started a ferry service between there and New York City. His steamboat *Jersey* took approximately fifteen minutes to cross the Hudson River. On July 4, Fulton's boat took part in a historic first, the transport of troops across water by steam-powered craft, as his "most excellent machine" ferried a battery of "flying artillery," headed for upstate New York, to Manhattan. It took four trips for the *Jersey* to get four guns, caissons, limbers, horses and men across the river.

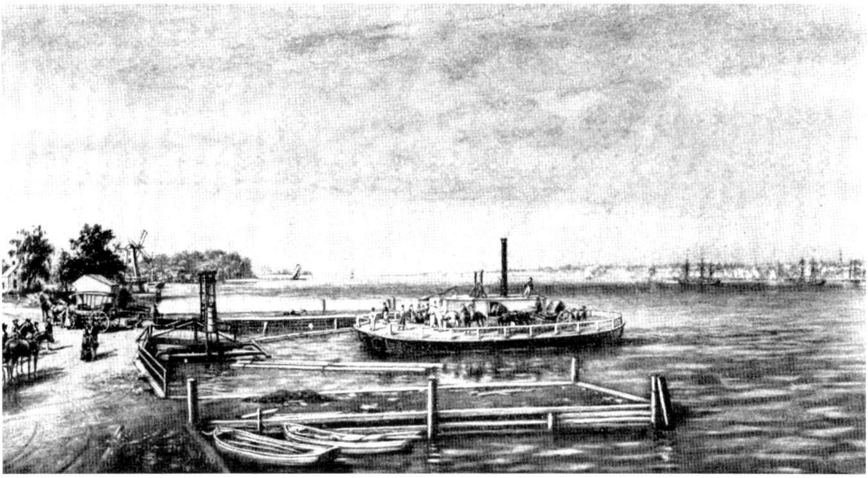

The Paulus Hook Ferry transported the first U.S. troops by steam power in 1812. *James M. Madden.*

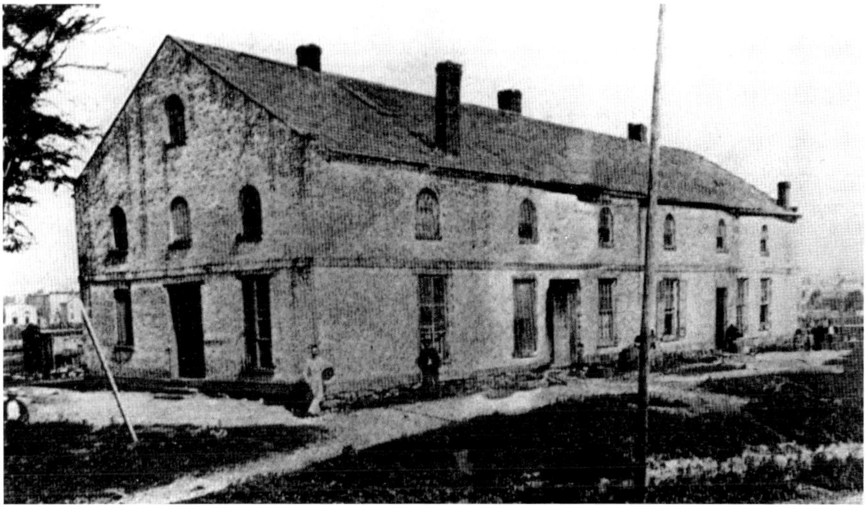

The arsenal building at Paulus Hook was used to store supplies during the War of 1812. *James M. Madden.*

Following the declaration of war against Great Britain, Federalists, hoping to gain pacifist Quaker votes, re-christened themselves as the "Friends of Peace." A disgruntled Jeffersonian Republican threatened a Federalist newspaper, Elizabeth's *Essex Patriot*, in a message warning, "Your damd tory paper will be serve a Baltimore trick if don't quit printing federal lies. If your shop burn down…tis not any more than what you deserve." The antiwar paper's office was indeed torched on October 20, 1813.

On December 29, Princeton-born naval officer Commodore William Bainbridge, commanding the iconic ship USS *Constitution*, decisively defeated HMS *Java* off the coast of Brazil. Although Bainbridge was wounded twice himself, the fight demonstrated his men's superior training and marksmanship with both artillery and small arms.

## 1813

New Jersey–born Zebulon Pike, noted explorer and army officer, was promoted to brigadier general in March but lost his life following the capture of York, Canada, when a powder magazine exploded as he sat atop it on April 27.

A British landing party reportedly skirmished with militiamen near Leesburg in Cumberland County on May 30.

On June 1, Burlington-born captain James Lawrence, a hero of the war against the Barbary pirates, sailed the USS *Chesapeake* out of Boston Harbor to battle HMS *Shannon*. Lawrence's crew was not yet trained properly, and the *Shannon* won the brief engagement, during which Lawrence was mortally wounded and gained eternal fame for his words, "Don't give up the ship." They did.

On June 4, Captain Lawrence, a prisoner of war, died from the wounds he received on June 1. Initially buried at Halifax with full military honors by the British, he was later reinterred at Trinity Church Cemetery in New York City, the burial place of Alexander Hamilton.

On July 4, an American subterfuge of hiding an armed party of sailors below decks on a local fishing boat, the *Yankee*, succeeded in capturing the British schooner *Eagle* off Sandy Hook.

On July 30, the Weymouth Furnace iron forge clerk noted, "Miss Woolfield beat Dan Beaty with broomstick as he was taken to hard drinking."

On August 17, "Andruss' detachment," composed of militia companies from Hunterdon, Middlesex, Sussex, Monmouth and Essex Counties, left the New Jersey militia base at Paulus Hook en route to garrison Fort Richmond on Staten Island. They remained on duty there through September 25. The New Jersey militia spent the War of 1812 as rotating service garrison troops for various coastal defense positions, most notably Sandy Hook, the gateway to New York Harbor. New Jersey contributed a little over six thousand men to the war effort, mostly militiamen deployed for brief periods. The Fifteenth United States Infantry, a regular army regiment recruited by Zebulon Pike in New Jersey, took part in the invasion of Canada and was known in the army as "the New Jersey regiment."

On November 13, William Franklin, son of Benjamin and last royal governor of New Jersey, died in England.

The library founded in 1796 and maintained by the state government in Trenton was officially named the New Jersey State Library.

# 1814

On April 1, the Martha Furnace clerk recorded the events of a militia drill at Bodine's tavern in his diary: "Captain Townsend was so intoxicated that he did not know the duty of a Captain. At length they had a courtmarshal [*sic*] over him."

On July 30, the Martha Furnace clerk recorded in his diary: "Solomon Truax and E. Hambleton was married this evening. Had a great time, ended of kissing the Bride & others some taking gates off the hinges and throwing them in the woods, and some to quarreling."

The Treaty of Ghent, ending the War of 1812, was signed on December 24.

The Decataur Powder Mill exploded in an "earthquakelike rumbling."

# 1815

The Treaty of Ghent was ratified by the U.S. Senate on February 16.

On June 2, Philip Kearny, nineteenth-century New Jersey's greatest war hero, was born in New York City. He would spend most of his formative years on a family estate near Newark.

Inventor Seth Boyden arrived in Newark from Foxborough, Massachusetts, bringing a leather-splitting machine along with him. Boyden was a remarkable figure, a mechanical genius and polymath inventor with an "indifference to money" who created such diverse products as patent leather, a hat-forming machine, steam engines and strawberry hybrids, as well as producing the first daguerreotype photograph in the United States.

Regular travel service by sloop was initiated between Philadelphia and the growing resort town of Cape May.

## 1816

The year was called the year of the "cold summer" when recorded temperatures were well below normal for the season.

The first bank in South Jersey below Cooper's Ferry (today's Camden) opened in Bridge Town (today's Bridgeton).

Napoleon Bonaparte's brother Joseph bought the Point Breeze estate at Bordentown. He lived there until 1839.

It was revealed that the Colt family owned 1,991 of the SUM's 2,620 shares.

## 1817

The Hammond Town (today's Hammonton) glassworks was established by William Coffin and Jonathan Haines. Coffin named it for his son, James Hammond Coffin.

## 1818

The Vail Iron Works at Speedwell in Morristown built machinery for the ship *Savannah*, the first vessel to cross the Atlantic Ocean under partial steam power.

On November 18, in Jersey City, Louis Charles Guille ascended in a balloon and, at five hundred feet, cut his line to the ground and jumped out, using a primitive version of the parachute. He landed safely, in the first recorded parachute jump in America.

Following the discovery of a plot to sell Middlesex County slaves and kidnapped free African Americans in New Orleans, legislation was passed forbidding the sale of slaves outside the state.

## 1819

Newark inventor Seth Boyden perfected a method to make patent leather.

Pierre Berthier, a French scientist, named the zinc ore found at Franklin, New Jersey, "Franklinite."

## 1820

The census reported New Jersey's population as 277,575, a 13 percent increase over 1810.

Sussex County's population of 32,754 people made it the most populous county in the state.

A poorhouse was established on the oddly shaped "Snake Hill" that jutted out of the Meadowlands in today's Hudson County. Much of the original hill has been ground down over the years, but it remains a striking sight from the roads leading to New York City.

## 1821

William Still was reportedly born in October or November (other sources list his birthday in 1819) in Medford to former slaves Levin and Charity Still. William had little formal education but moved to Philadelphia and began to work for an abolitionist society. He rose to be a leader in the movement and wrote a history of the Underground Railroad. William's daughter Caroline was a graduate of the Women's Medical College of Philadelphia, and his brother James, a self-taught physician, was known as the "Black Doctor of the Pines."

## 1822

Timothy Webster was born in Newhaven, England, on March 12. Webster immigrated with his family to Princeton, New Jersey, at the age of eight and lived there until he became a detective for the Pinkerton agency in

1853. With the outbreak of the Civil War, he served as a Union spy but was discovered, tried, convicted and hanged in Richmond in 1862, the first American hanged as a spy since Nathan Hale.

The former Brotherton Reservation Indians moved from the Oneida reservation in New York to Wisconsin.

Morristown resident and businessman George Macculloch proposed a canal across northern New Jersey, using the abundant water supply provided by Lake Hopatcong.

Naturalist Constantine Samuel Rafinesque claimed to have discovered the Walam Olum, which he asserted was a series of pictograph tablets describing the ancient history of New Jersey's Lenape Native Americans. In 1833, he produced what he said was a translation of the pictographs, detailing the Lenape journey from Asia to America. The translation was a source of much controversy over the years, with historians and anthropologists arguing over its authenticity. In 1993, however, the Walam Olum was conclusively proved to be fraudulent, and scholars concluded that Rafinesque forged it in an attempt to win the Paris Prix Volney essay contest of 1834.

John Colt became the first manufacturer to substitute cotton for linen in sailcloth in his Paterson factory.

# 1823

By the end of the year, there were three large woolen factories and two factories making cotton "duck" cloth for sails at Paterson.

Salem County farmer Job Tyler shipped a massive ox to Philadelphia via special steamboat. A brass band led the unfortunate animal through the streets to a slaughter point, where it was established that it yielded 2,111 pounds of beef, 365 pounds of tallow and 176 pounds of hide.

The first lightship was anchored seven miles off Sandy Hook.

# 1824

Warren County was created out of Sussex County and named for Dr. Joseph Warren, a Revolutionary War hero killed at Bunker Hill.

Hunterdon County farmer Michael Floy developed a peach hybrid he named the "George IV" in honor of the king of England. It was recognized as a new variety by the London Horticultural Society.

The significant legal case of *Gibbons v. Ogden* was decided. New Jersey steamboat operator and former governor Aaron Ogden had asked the State of New York, which had licensed his route to New York City from Elizabeth, to forbid his former partner Thomas Gibbons from running the same route. The case went to the United States Supreme Court, which decided in favor of Gibbons, citing federal, rather than state, authority over interstate commerce.

John Stevens completed construction of an experimental "steam wagon" and ran it on a circular track at a speed of twelve miles an hour in Hoboken.

## 1825

A steamboat service was established between Bridgeton and Philadelphia.

Belvidere was named the county seat of Warren County.

A three-thousand-seat amphitheater in Jersey City hosted bull baiting contests every Friday, as crowds gathered to watch "the sport afforded by bulls, bears, buffaloes and dogs fighting." A Jersey City newspaper claimed most of the spectators were from New York.

The Jersey Porcelain and Earthenware Company was established in Jersey City and would produce pottery through 1892. The company used the English method of transfer printing in decoration for the first time in America, and its goods were considered of very high quality.

Queen's College, which had closed once more for lack of funds in 1821, reopened on November 14 as Rutgers College. New Yorker Henry Rutgers contributed $5,000 and a new bell to the school that now bore his name.

Construction began on George Macculloch's canal, to be called the Morris Canal.

## 1826

Newark inventor Seth Boyden moved on from patent leather and produced the first malleable iron made in America.

## 1827

On September 30, Paterson cotton millworker Sam Patch jumped off a bridge over the Paterson falls into the Passaic River and survived. It was the beginning of Patch's brief career as a professional daredevil, in which he jumped from ship masts and over falls until his death.

## 1828

Cooper's Ferry residents seceded from Newton Township and created the town of Camden.

The Hunterdon County Courthouse was built in Greek Revival style in Flemington. It was the venue for the Lindbergh baby kidnapping trial of Bruno Richard Hauptmann in 1935 and still stands today.

A dock was built at Long Branch, enabling vacationers to travel to the increasingly popular resort by boat.

## 1829

On Friday, November 13, at Genesee Falls, New York, daredevil Sam Patch made his last jump. After hitting the water, he never resurfaced.

## 1830

The census reported that New Jersey's population was 320,823, a 15.6 percent increase over 1820. There were still 2,246 slaves in the state.

Mary Mapes was born on January 26. As Mary Mapes Dodge, a Newark widow who became the sole supporter of her family, she wrote the vastly popular children's book *Hans Brinker, or The Silver Skates* and became editor of *Saint Nicholas Magazine for Boys and Girls*, the premier children's literary publication of the nineteenth century, in 1872.

In March, a local farmer discovered Sam Patch's body under river ice several miles from where he had made his final jump four months earlier. Patch's grave marker was inscribed: "Here lies Sam Patch, Such is Fame."

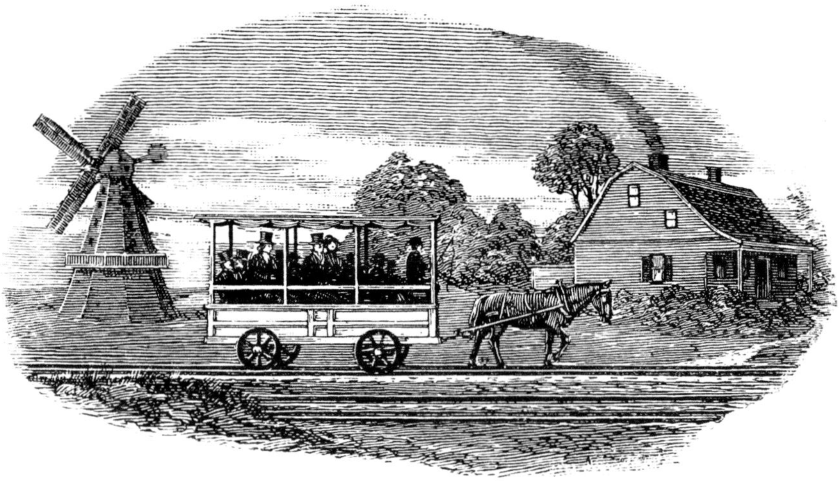

The first New Jersey railroad—drawn by horse power. *James M. Madden.*

On September 9, Charles Durant flew in a balloon from New York City to Perth Amboy.

The Gentlemen's Powder Mill in Spotswood, a plant dedicated to making high-grade gunpowder for sport hunters—the powder can bore a picture of a gentleman in a frock coat and high hat—exploded.

Dr. Samuel Fowler of Franklin perfected a process of making a zinc oxide powder serve as a paint base.

Robert L. and Edwin Stevens became president and treasurer of the Camden and Amboy Railroad, intended to be a horse-drawn rail route between Camden and Perth Amboy. Robert traveled to England to study the layout of railroad tracks and also to investigate the use of a steam engine in place of the horses.

## 1831

On November 12, the first test movement by steam power on a railroad in the state of New Jersey occurred on a segment of the Camden and Amboy Railroad line in Bordentown. The power was supplied by the imported English steam locomotive John Bull. The John Bull is currently in the Smithsonian Institute collection.

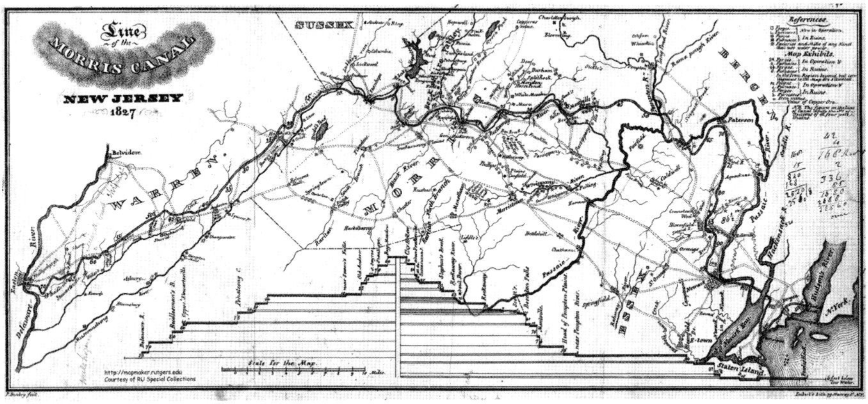


The route of the Morris Canal. *Wickimedia Commons.*

The Camden and Amboy Railroad merged with the Delaware and Raritan Canal Company, forming the Joint Companies.

The Elizabethtown and Somerville and Paterson and Hudson River Railroads were chartered by the state.

The Morris Canal, connecting Newark and Phillipsburg, opened. The canal route, employing a system of locks and inclined planes, rose 913 feet on its way west from Newark to Lake Hopatcong and then descended 760 feet to Phillipsburg on the Delaware River.

## 1832

In March, the *Newark Daily Advertiser*, the state's first daily newspaper, began publication.

The New Jersey legislature appropriated $2,000, funds acquired from the sale of the former Brotherton reservation land, to pay to tribal representatives of the former Brotherton Indians. Among the representatives was Bartholomew Calvin, a College of New Jersey graduate and son of the Native American schoolmaster at Brotherton.

The New Jersey state legislature granted a monopoly to the Joint Companies on transportation across the state between New York and Philadelphia. In turn, the state received two thousand shares of company stock and some taxes. The company guaranteed the state an income of at least $30,000 a year, allowing the legislators to depend less on property and other taxes for revenue.

William Dunlap's *History of the American Theater*, the first work of its kind, was published.

# 1833

On September 6, Antoine le Blanc, a French immigrant, was hanged in Morristown after being convicted of murdering his employer, Samuel Sayre, along with Mrs. Sayre and their servant Phoebe. It was claimed that ten thousand people attended the public hanging. Following his death, le Blanc's body was used for scientific experiments, after which his corpse was skinned and tanned for making wallets, book jackets and lampshades.

On November 8, two months after steam locomotives replaced horsepower on the Camden and Amboy railroad, an axle-bearing journal box on an engine traveling thirty-five miles an hour in Hightstown overheated, and the oily rags used to reduce friction caught fire, causing a broken axle on one of the cars. The train derailed and overturned, and of twenty-four passengers aboard, only one escaped injury. One man was killed and another later died of his injuries. Among the casualties was Cornelius Vanderbilt, who broke a leg and vowed never to travel by train again. Ironically, he later became the owner of the New York Central Railroad. The one uninjured passenger was congressman and former U.S. president John Quincy Adams, who referred to the accident as "the most dreadful catastrophe that ever my eyes beheld." The train wreck is the earliest one recorded in the United States that involved the death of passengers.

The *Newark Daily Advertiser* reported that Robert Stevens was promoting the use of anthracite coal rather than wood as fuel for his Camden and Amboy Railroad engines.

# 1834

The Delaware and Raritan Canal was completed between Trenton and New Brunswick.

An African American minister, Reverend Samuel Cornish, then resident in Belleville, established the Newark Anti-Slavery Society. Cornish later served as pastor of the First African/Plane Street Presbyterian Church in Newark.

Ironmaster William Henry successfully introduced a revolutionary new hot blast furnace in his forge at Oxford. The method increased production by 40 percent and cut fuel use in half.

The state had 61 miles of railroad tracks at the end of the year. The high point year in railroad track mileage in New Jersey was 1920, with 2,353 miles.

## 1835

On June 19, a tornado swept across Middlesex County, crossing the state from Amwell and roaring down George Street, killing two people and seriously damaging houses before moving down the Raritan River and finally ending on Staten Island. A young boy was carried into the air from his George Street residence and deposited two hundred yards away in Burnet Street, suffering only minor injuries.

On July 20, over two thousand Paterson textile workers from twenty mills went on strike demanding a reduction in work hours from thirteen and a half to eleven hours a day. The mill owners refused to negotiate but did reduce hours to twelve hours a day on weekdays and nine hours on Saturdays. The workers returned to work, but the strike leaders were blacklisted by employers.

The Morris and Essex Railroad was chartered by the State of New Jersey.

A fire in a German boardinghouse in Newark spread rapidly and burned down a block of houses before it was brought under control.

The first commercial cranberry bog was established by Benjamin Thomas near Burr's Mills in Burlington County.

The Camden Race Course was built on the White Horse Pike near Haddon Heights.

In the wake of protests regarding a public hanging in Mount Holly that drew ten thousand jovial spectators and liquor and gambling tents, the state legislature passed a law remanding executions to jail grounds.

## 1836

On November 19, the Morris and Essex Railroad began passenger service between Morristown and Orange. The horse-drawn car made two trips a day, and the cost was fifteen cents each way.

Samuel Colt patented his revolving-cylinder repeating firearm and established production facilities at a factory in the Colt family stronghold of Paterson, which provided the popular name of the gun: the Paterson Model.

The Morris Canal was extended from Newark to Jersey City.

The value of leather goods produced in Newark during the year was $3,500,000, which was half the value of the city's total industrial output.

The New Jersey state prison, designed by prison architect John Haviland, was opened in Trenton.

## 1837

On March 18, Grover Cleveland, twenty-second and twenty-fourth president of the United States, the only president to serve two nonconsecutive terms, was born in Caldwell.

The first Colt revolvers were produced in Paterson.

Passaic and Atlantic Counties were created, Passaic from parts of Bergen and Essex and Atlantic from the eastern section of Gloucester County.

Thomas Rogers built a locomotive called the Sandusky in Paterson. It was the first in a long line of railroad engines manufactured in the city, which became the leading locomotive production site in the country for the remainder of the century. The Sandusky introduced the steam whistle to railroading.

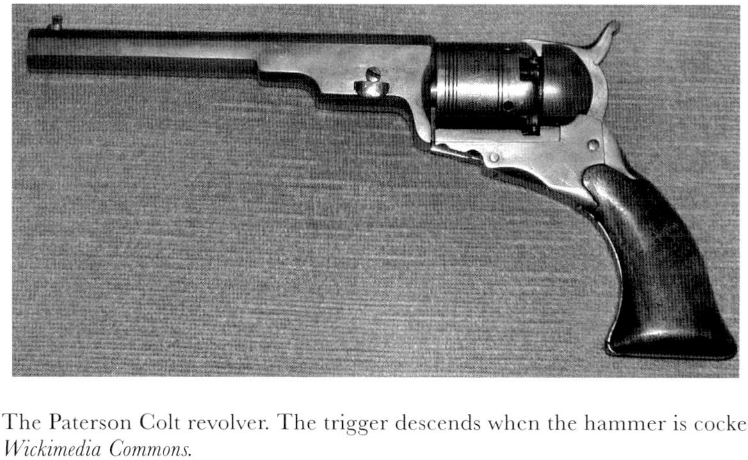

The Paterson Colt revolver. The trigger descends when the hammer is cocked. *Wickimedia Commons.*

The Panic of 1837, caused by bank speculation and a collapsing real estate bubble, created a fiscal crisis that led to a drop in prices and wages and a spike in unemployment—what would in the twentieth century be called a depression. The panic had a serious detrimental effect on New Jersey industry, which was just starting to develop. Fortunately, the state was still basically agrarian, and many men thrown out of work were able to return to family farms to survive.

## 1838

On January 6, 1838, Samuel F.B. Morse and Alfred Vail demonstrated the telegraph for the first time at Speedwell Iron Works in Morristown. The first message sent read: "A patient waiter is no loser."

On February 22, Jersey City was officially incorporated. Dudley S. Gregory became the first mayor.

The Delaware and Raritan Canal was extended to Bordentown.

Mercer County was created from parts of Hunterdon, Somerset, Middlesex and Burlington Counties. It was named for General Hugh Mercer, mortally wounded at the Battle of Princeton.

The logbook entry for the whaling ship *Wells*, one of two sailing from Newark, reads: "At 3 P.M. saw sperm whale. Starboard boat first got fast then lost whale. Larbord boat got fast, but whale stove [broke] boat and killed Abner Coffin, First officer, aged 26." Newark was a minor whaling port from about 1832 to 1840.

The Broad Seal War erupted when Governor William Pennington certified members of his Whig Party with his "broad seal," or certificate of legitimacy, as official winners of the congressional elections held that year, even though it was evident that at least some of the Democratic candidates had clearly won. The House of Representatives resolved the issue by seating the Democrats who had actually won the election.

## 1839

Christopher Colt opened the first silk mill in Paterson.

The first public high school in the state was opened in Newark.

In August, while on a visit to Long Beach Island, Dr. William Newell of Allentown witnessed the wreck of the ship *Count Perasto* on a sand bar three hundred yards from shore. The crew of twelve men all drowned, as Newell and others watched in helpless horror, for they could do nothing. Newell subsequently vowed that he would do something to assist the victims of shipwrecks.

## 1840

The census reported New Jersey's population as 373,306, a 16.4 percent increase over 1830.

Cornelia Hancock, the Civil War nurse known as the "Florence Nightingale of America" for her work, was born at Hancock's Bridge on February 8. After the Civil War, Hancock became an educator and pioneering social worker. She lived a long, fruitful and socially useful life before dying in Atlantic City in 1927.

Hudson County was created from parts of Bergen and Essex Counties.

Peter Ballantine opened a brewery in Newark to provide beer for the city's growing German population. Ironically, Ballantine was a Scotsman.

English immigrant John Ryle arrived in Paterson to take over a failed attempt at silk making at a factory purchased by George W. Murray. Ryle succeeded where others failed and is considered the father of the Paterson silk industry.

The African American community of Snow Hill (today's Lawnside) was founded in Camden County.

The New Jersey State Anti-Slavery Society was formed.

## 1841

On May 8, Revolutionary War veteran Samuel Sutphen died at the age of ninety-four. Sutphen, a slave, substituted for his master, Caspar Berger, for several tours of duty in both the militia and the New Jersey Continental Line between 1776 and 1780. He fought in numerous engagements, including the Battle of Long Island, and he was present at the Battles of Princeton and Monmouth and was wounded in a New York State skirmish with

British troops following his return from the 1779 campaign against the Iroquois Indians. He later gained his freedom. The federal government denied Sutphen a veteran pension in 1832 because he was a slave when he served. The State of New Jersey, however, did grant him a special pension for his service.

The first Fresnel lens used in a lighthouse in the United States was installed at Navesink Lighthouse on Beacon Hill in Highlands, the location of today's "twin lights." The lens, developed in 1822 by French engineer Augustin Fresnel, used a series of prisms to collect and concentrate generated light and dramatically increase brightness.

## 1842

On March 9, the New Jersey legislature abolished imprisonment for debt.

Production ceased at Samuel Colt's Paterson firearms factory, which went out of business after producing 1,450 revolving rifles and carbines, 462 revolving shotguns and 2,350 handguns. Guns assembled from previously manufactured parts continued to be sold through 1847, to satisfy Colt's debts. The revolver inventor would successfully revive his business in Hartford, Connecticut, in 1848.

## 1843

On August 31, Phineas T. Barnum staged a "Grand Buffalo Hunt" in Hoboken. In what was called a "humbug" in those days, he had a costumed mounted man chase some buffalo around a fenced field. When some animals broke loose and stampeded, a spectator was killed falling out of a tree, but fortunately for Barnum, liability lawsuits were not yet in fashion. It was the promoter's first big show, and it launched his career.

A group of families from Albany, New York, purchased the Van Mater farm in Middletown and founded the "North American Phalanx," an idealistic quasi-socialist self-sustaining community inspired by the social and economic dysfunction that followed in the wake of the Panic of 1837. The community was based on the writings of Albert Brisbane, which were, in turn, inspired by the work of French social theorist

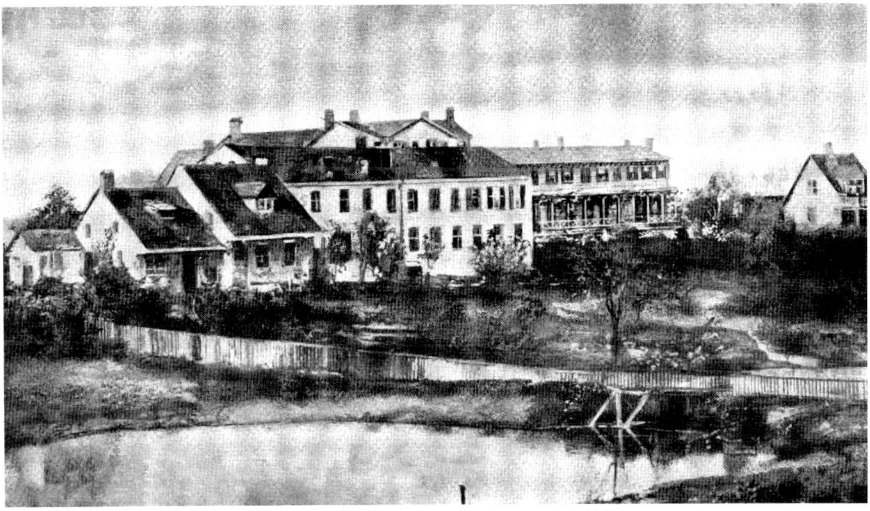

The utopian North American Phalanx community as it appeared in 1850. From Kull, *History of New Jersey.*

Charles Fourier. Internal disputes led to the closing of the community over the winter of 1855–56.

Boat builder Joseph Francis of Toms River developed an interest in saving lives in shipwrecks and designed a corrugated iron lifeboat to be used in lifesaving operations.

## 1844

On January 25, George Ashby was born in Burlington, New Jersey. Ashby, an African American, would serve as a sergeant in the Forty-fifth United States Colored Infantry during the Civil War from 1864 to 1865. He would outlive every other New Jersey Civil War veteran.

In February, Princeton-born navy captain Robert Stockton, grandson of New Jersey Declaration of Independence signer Richard Stockton, took his ship *Princeton* for a pleasure cruise on the Potomac River, with President John Tyler, his cabinet and two hundred guests aboard. A cannon designed by Stockton was fired several times to entertain the guests before it exploded and killed six people, including Secretary of State Abel Upshur, Secretary of the Navy Thomas Gilmer and the president's soon to be father-in-law, as well as his personal valet. A quickly held court of inquiry absolved Stockton, a personal friend of the president, from all blame.

On June 3, Garret "Gus" Hobart was born in Long Branch. Hobart became a successful and very wealthy attorney and rose through the crony culture of nineteenth-century New Jersey politics, serving in the legislature and as chairman of the Republican State Committee. He was the Republican vice presidential nominee in 1896 and then vice president of the United States. Hobart died of an apparent heart attack in 1899 and was replaced on the Republican ticket by Theodore Roosevelt in the election of 1900. Had he not died, Hobart would have ascended to the presidency when President McKinley was assassinated in 1901.

A new New Jersey state constitution was drawn up and then approved by public referendum. It replaced the constitution of 1776 and provided for popular election of the governor for a three-year term. The governor had previously been elected by the legislature for a one-year term. Other reforms in the new constitution included a clearer separation of judicial, legislative and executive powers, although the governor did share some judicial responsibilities.

Camden County was created from Gloucester County.

Dorothea Lynd Dix began to petition for improvements in the New Jersey prison system and the establishment of an asylum for the mentally ill.

Joseph Francis invented an unsinkable life-car to evacuate people from shipwrecks safely.

# 1845

George C. Stratton, a former congressman and member of the Whig Party, was the first governor inaugurated for a three-year term under the constitution of 1844.

Peter Cooper and Abram Hewitt founded the Trenton Iron Company to fill contracts for rails for the Camden and Amboy Railroad.

The New Jersey Historical Society was established.

Mutual Benefit Life Insurance Company was founded in Newark.

Steamboat service between Bridgeton and Philadelphia began on a regular basis.

Dorothea Dix's New Jersey campaign for a state mental hospital culminated with the state senate and assembly passing a law establishing the State Lunatic Asylum, to be built in Ewing Township.

A baseball game, in which the New York Club defeated the Brooklyn Club by a score of twenty-four to four, was played at Elysian Fields in Hoboken on October 21. This contest was prior to the June 19, 1846 game that is usually cited as the date of the first game played at Elysian Field or in New Jersey. In the latter contest, the New York Club defeated the Knickerbocker Base Ball Club of New York by a score of twenty-three to one.

## 1846

On April 25, the United States declared war on Mexico.

On May 22, Governor Stratton responded to a request from President Polk for troops to fight in the Mexican War with a proclamation calling on "organized uniform companies and other citizens of the state to enroll themselves" in the regiment. The response was underwhelming, as the enthusiasm of Jerseymen for actually fighting in the Mexican War was, as in much of the Northeast, minimal. No troops were supplied.

On August 18, Newark-born general Stephen Watts Kearny, commander of the Army of the West, a less-than-impressive collection of Missouri mounted volunteer units; the Mormon Battalion; and some artillery, stiffened by his own dragoon regiment, captured Santa Fe, New Mexico, without a shot being fired.

Slavery was formally abolished in New Jersey. Children born of enslaved people were no longer bound to apprenticeship. Those people in servitude prior to the 1804 gradual abolition act had their legal statuses changed to "apprentices for life "and were granted certain legal rights.

Dr. William Newell was elected to Congress.

## 1847

Thomas Alva Edison was born in Milan, Ohio, on February 11. Edison would become the most prolific American inventor and marketer of inventions, most of which were developed in New Jersey, initially in Menlo Park and later in his West Orange laboratories.

In April, the United States government again requested that New Jersey provide soldiers for the war with Mexico.

In April and May, three companies of the Tenth United States Infantry, a regular army regiment, were recruited in New Jersey and shipped out to Matamoros, Mexico, where they served on occupation duty.

Henry Clay visited Cape May in August, seeking a place to mourn for his son, killed the previous February at the Mexican War Battle of Buena Vista. Word of his visit leaked out, however, and he was mobbed by admirers on his August 16 arrival.

On September 29, four companies of New Jersey volunteers left for Vera Cruz, Mexico, where they served on occupation duty for the next nine months.

Harrison Woodhull Crosby of Jamesburg became the first person to successfully pack tomatoes in a tin can.

William Colgate moved his soap factory from New York to Jersey City.

Joseph Dixon moved his crucible steel factory to Jersey City from Salem, Massachusetts.

The Cunard Company established a dock in Jersey City.

The Camden Race Course, plagued by what historian John Cunningham called "drunkenness, gambling and debauchery," closed.

African American New Jerseyan William Still began working for the Pennsylvania Society for the Abolition of Slavery in Philadelphia.

## 1848

On January 21, Captain Joshua W. Collet of Company H, Tenth United States Infantry, a unit raised in New Jersey for service in the Mexican War, was killed in a duel with another American officer, Captain Alexander Wilkin of New York, at Camargo, Mexico. He was the only New Jersey officer commanding troops recruited in New Jersey to die in the war.

On February 2, the Mexican War officially ended with the signing of the Treaty of Guadalupe Hidalgo.

On May 23, William E. Sackett was born in New York City. As a journalist, Sackett specialized in New Jersey politics, writing for both the *New York Times* and the *New York Herald*. His *Modern Battles of Trenton*, two volumes on the state's political struggles from 1866 to 1912, are classics of the genre. Sackett died on November 18, 1926.

On October 31, Newark's general Stephen Watts Kearny died in Saint Louis of yellow fever, which he had contracted in Mexico while serving as military governor of Vera Cruz. Kearny was buried in Belefontaine Cemetery in Saint Louis.

The first Jewish congregations in New Jersey met in Newark and Paterson.

The United States Life Saving Service was established through legislation introduced by New Jersey congressman and physician William A. Newell. The first two stations in New Jersey were built in today's Ocean (then part of Monmouth) County.

Charles Ewan founded the Ewansville Cider Works and Distillery, the largest distiller of apple brandy in New Jersey in the nineteenth century.

John A. Roebling moved his wire rope cable company to Trenton. Roebling's cables were a key component in the building of suspension bridges.

## 1849

Hoboken was classified as a township.

The Somerville and Easton Railroad purchased the Elizabethtown and Somerville Railroad and adopted a new name: the Central Railroad Company of New Jersey.

## 1850

According to the census, New Jersey's population was 489,555, a 31.1 percent increase over 1840. This was almost double the increase seen in any previous census and reflects the state's vastly increased immigration and industrialization.

New Jersey adjutant general Thomas McCall Cadwallader advised Governor Daniel Haines that the state militia was in a deplorable condition and that efforts must be made to "give life and energy to the [militia] system."

Ocean County was created from Monmouth County.

The Rogers locomotive plant in Paterson was turning out more than one hundred engines a year.

The *Ayrshire*, a Scottish ship, ran aground and lost its main mast and rudder in a storm off Absecon Beach in late December 1849. The ship drifted northward until it ran aground at Squan Beach (today's Manasquan) on January 12, 1850. Rescuers fired a line to the ship from a line-throwing mortar. The line was used to run a Joseph Francis–designed life-car that carried four people to safety. It was the first use of a life-car in a shipwreck rescue. Of the 202 passengers on the ship, all but 1 survived.

Chapter 5

# 1851 to 1900

## 1851

German American artist Emmanuel Gottlieb Leutze painted his iconic, if not altogether historically accurate, oil on canvas *Washington Crossing the Delaware*. The painting portrays General George Washington's crossing of the river from Pennsylvania to New Jersey prior to the Battle of Trenton on the night of December 25, 1776. The original painting, in the collection of a German museum, was destroyed in a World War II air raid. Leutze made a second copy, however, and it is in the collection of the Metropolitan Museum of Art in New York City.

## 1852

Clara Barton established the first free public school in New Jersey in Bordentown.

## 1853

A town meeting in Newton rejected the idea of raising money to provide for public schools, which, with the exception of the one established the year before in Bordentown, charged tuition.

A distraught Hoboken man attempted to commit suicide by jumping off the ferry *James Rumsey* in midstream on its way to New York. Saved by the captain, who had a lifeboat launched to scoop him out of the water, the man later disclosed that his motive was to escape his extreme poverty. The third suicide attempt off a ferry within a week, the incident led the *New York Times* to speculate, "The fashionable mode of suicide now-a-days appears to be jumping from the ferry-boats."

## 1854

On March 3, Atlantic City was incorporated.

On April 15, the ship *Powhattan* (aka *Powhatan*) ran aground about six miles south of the Harvey Cedars lifesaving station in a storm. The ship remained afloat until the following day and then broke apart, resulting in the deaths of the entire crew and passengers. The victims washed up on the beach as far south as Atlantic City and were buried in three cemeteries. Fifty-four were interred in a mass grave at Smithville Methodist Church and forty-five in Absecon. More bodies washed ashore at Peahala on Long Beach Island and were buried in paupers' graves in the Baptist cemetery in Manahawkin, where a monument was erected by the State of New Jersey in 1904 to honor the victims of the wreck. The *Powhatan* disaster served as an impetus for the building of the Absecon Lighthouse later in the year.

On November 14, another terrible shipwreck involving German immigrant passengers occurred when the *New Era* ran aground off Deal Beach near today's Asbury Park in a dense fog. Of 385 passengers and crew on board, only 163 were saved. In 1893, Asbury Park founder James A. Bradley placed a memorial monument to those lost on the *New Era* on the beach, but it has gone missing over the years. An attempt to find it in 2012 using ground-penetrating radar failed.

Fourteen-year-old Charles Hopkins began to assist his father, an Underground Railroad conductor, by escorting an escaped slave from one safe house to another in Morris County. Hopkins went on to fight in the Civil War and was awarded the Medal of Honor for his bravery at the Battle of Gaines' Mill in 1862.

Elizabethtown officially changed its name to the City of Elizabeth.

The Progressive coeducational and racially integrated Eagleswood School was established at the Raritan Bay Union utopian community. The school closed in 1861.

The Trenton Iron Company made the first iron I-beams for use in building construction.

## 1855

Trenton State Normal School was established to train teachers on February 9. The school became Trenton State Teachers' College in 1929, then Trenton State College in 1958 and the College of New Jersey in 1996.

One-armed New Jersey Mexican War hero Philip Kearny built "Kearny's Castle" on his Bellegrove estate.

A Camden and Amboy train missed a turnout at Burlington and backed up to avoid colliding with another train but hit a wagon crossing the tracks, derailing a number of cars. The casualty toll was high—twenty-four dead and over one hundred injured.

## 1856

A fire broke out on the steam ferry *New Jersey* as it headed across the Delaware River from Philadelphia to New Jersey on the night of March 15 with more than one hundred people on board. Ice in the river interfered with rescue operations, and more than sixty people died.

Seton Hall College was established by Catholic bishop James Roosevelt Bayley in Madison. The school moved to South Orange in 1860 and became a university in 1950.

## 1857

The Panic of 1857, the first international economic crisis in the modern era, began in Great Britain and spread to America, where insurance companies, banks and railroads overinvested in artificially inflated western land went bankrupt as values dramatically dropped. Newark, a booming industrial town at the time, suffered severely, and the bottom fell out of its economy, leaving people literally starving in the streets. Newark did not begin a comeback until its economy was stimulated by extensive government spending on leather goods and clothing in the Civil War.

Unlike in 1837, when the laboring force of cities like Newark had some connection with the countryside in a far more rural society, the working classes in 1857, many of them immigrants, were in dire straits. On November 18, two thousand unemployed workers held a mass meeting in Newark's Military Park, demanding jobs that were not forthcoming.

Nominated for governor by a joint convention of the American Party (also known as the anti-immigrant Know-Nothing Party) and the new Republican Party, William A. Newell was elected governor in November 1856, assuming office in January 1857. In his role as governor under the constitution of 1844, Newell presided over the court of pardons, which embroiled him in a controversy when medical student James P. Donnelly was convicted of murdering Alfred S. Moses at a Monmouth County hotel over a gambling debt and sentenced to death. New Jersey's Irish Catholics, a growing segment of the state's population, contended that Donnelly was framed and convicted by a Protestant legal establishment. Newell cast a vote against commuting Donnelly's sentence to life imprisonment, and the governor, already suspect due to his anti-immigrant public policies, gained the undying enmity of the state's Irish community, damaging his future political prospects.

## 1858

Richard Esterbrook emigrated from England to New Jersey and established the Esterbrook steel pen factory in Camden.

## 1859

Princeton undergraduates threatened one another with handguns during a particularly stormy college election.

The Cape May Lighthouse was constructed.

Charles S. Olden was elected governor of New Jersey, running as the candidate of the "Opposition Party," an ad hoc coalition of Republican, Whig and American or "Know-Nothing" party members.

# 1860

The census of 1860 reported 672,035 people living in New Jersey.

Charles Clark of Pilesgrove in Salem County raised fifty-two hogs weighing over five hundred pounds each.

In the presidential election of 1860, New Jersey split its electoral vote, giving four votes to Stephen Douglas and three to Abraham Lincoln. This was due to confusion among supporters of Lincoln's several Democratic opponents, as he received only 58,346 votes out of 121,215 cast.

In December, in a skirmish known as the "Battle of Pine Swamp," the armed citizens of Timbuctoo, an African American community near Mount Holly, forcibly resisted the attempt of "slave catchers" from Philadelphia to capture an escaped slave named Perry Simmons.

# 1861

On January 9, John McGowan of Elizabeth, a former Revenue Marine (today's Coast Guard) officer who had established lifesaving stations along the New Jersey coast, sailed the unarmed ship *Star of the West* into Charleston Harbor on a mission to resupply Fort Sumter, then besieged by South Carolina secessionists. When his vessel was hit by two rounds from a shore battery, McGowan withdrew. Some count these as the first shots of the Civil War.

On February 21, president-elect Abraham Lincoln arrived in New Jersey on his way to Washington. Lincoln spoke a few words at brief stops in Jersey City, Newark, Elizabeth, Rahway, New Brunswick and Princeton Junction, where a group of students from the College of New Jersey serenaded him. He moved on to Trenton, arriving there at noon and delivering short speeches to the State Senate and Assembly, and then left by train for Philadelphia at 2:30 p.m.

On April 12, Confederate forces fired on Fort Sumter in Charleston Harbor, igniting the Civil War. Despite New Jersey governor Charles S. Olden's previously expressed desire for compromise, reflecting the views of a fairly large number of New Jerseyans, the people of the state rallied to the Union cause in the wake of the attack.

On April 15, President Abraham Lincoln called for seventy-five thousand militiamen for three months' service. New Jersey's quota was four regiments.

On May 3, the men of New Jersey's Militia Brigade sailed out of Trenton down the Delaware River on their way to Washington. Some militiamen celebrated by firing their handguns in the air, and one Jersey City soldier from the Second Militia Regiment accidentally shot another soldier. The Jerseyans were the first full brigade to arrive in Washington.

On June 28, the First, Second and Third Regiments of New Jersey Volunteer Infantry, composing the First New Jersey Brigade, enlisted for three years' service, left Trenton for Washington by train. The Jersey boys smuggled three women aboard and "got drunk as the devil" on the way.

On August 7, General Philip Kearny, hero of the Mexican War, assumed command of the First New Jersey Brigade.

On October 5, Mayor Edmund T. Carpenter of Hudson City (now a part of Jersey City) was accidently bayoneted five or six times as he attempted to break up a riot in the Five Corners section between local citizens and German American soldiers of the Fifty-fourth New York Infantry Regiment, which was quartered in the city. Carpenter died of his wounds on Thanksgiving Day, the only public official to die of bayonet wounds in state history.

## 1862

On January 15, Colonel Joseph W. Allen and surgeon Frederick S. Weller of the Ninth New Jersey Volunteer Infantry were drowned when the small boat they were riding in was swamped during operations off Cape Hatteras, North Carolina. They were the first New Jersey officers to die in the Civil War.

On February 8, on Roanoke Island, North Carolina, the Ninth New Jersey Volunteer Infantry was the first New Jersey unit engaged in a battle, as opposed to a skirmish, in the Civil War. The regiment successfully charged through a swamp, gaining the nickname "Jersey Muskrats," and losing nine men killed and twenty-five wounded in the fight. Among the dead was Captain Joseph Henry of Oxford Furnace, the first New Jersey officer killed in action in the Civil War.

On May 4, the Second New Jersey Brigade, comprising the Fifth, Sixth, Seventh and Eighth New Jersey Volunteer Infantry Regiments, fought its first battle in a driving rainstorm at Williamsburg, Virginia, losing 536 men killed, wounded and missing.

On June 6, the First New Jersey Cavalry was ambushed in the Shenandoah Valley and suffered forty casualties, including Colonel Percy Wyndham, who was captured, and Captain Thomas Ryerson Haines, son of former New Jersey governor Daniel Haines, who was killed in action.

On June 27, the First New Jersey Brigade, then comprising the First, Second, Third and Fourth New Jersey Volunteer Infantry Regiments, fought its first major engagement at Gaines Mill, Virginia. Of the 2,300 men the brigade brought to the battle, 1,072 were killed, wounded or captured.

On July 7, President Lincoln called for "300,000 more" volunteers to help put down the Rebellion. New Jersey's quota was five regiments, or around 5,000 men, and included the Eleventh, Twelfth, Thirteen, Fourteenth and Fifteenth New Jersey Volunteer Infantry Regiments.

On August 12, Amos Alonzo Stagg, pioneer football coach and tackling dummy inventor, was born in Orange (in today's West Orange).

In August, the Federal government issued another call for troops, this one for men to serve nine months' active duty. New Jersey's quota was 10,478 men, which the state furnished in the form of eleven regiments, the Twenty-first through the Thirty-first New Jersey Volunteer Infantry regiments. The vast majority of these men were volunteers, but a few in a town that did not promise a modest bounty were draftees.

On August 25, sixteen-year-old Ellis Hamilton of Camden was commissioned a second lieutenant in the Fifteenth New Jersey Volunteer Infantry, making him the youngest commissioned officer in the Union army in the Civil War. Hamilton was subsequently promoted to first lieutenant and captain, before being mortally wounded at the Battle of the Wilderness on May 6, 1864. He died at a hospital in Georgetown ten days later.

On September 1, at Chantilly, Virginia, General Philip Kearny was killed while making a reconnaissance of Confederate lines. He was initially buried in New York's Trinity Churchyard but was reinterred in Arlington National Cemetery in 1912.

On September 17, the Thirteenth New Jersey Volunteer Infantry, in the army less than a month, fought in its first battle at Antietam Creek, Maryland, a few days after leaving Newark. Thrown into the hottest part of the battle, the Thirteenth suffered 101 casualties.

Joseph Wharton established the country's first nickel-processing plant in Camden. It remained the sole production site for nickel for the remainder of the nineteenth century.

Most of the New Jersey regiments in the Army of the Potomac were present at the disastrous Battle of Fredericksburg on December 13. Some units suffered heavy losses, including the Twenty-fourth New Jersey Volunteer Infantry, with 136 casualties, and the Twenty-eighth New Jersey Volunteer Infantry, with 193.

# 1863

As with Fredericksburg, most of the New Jersey soldiers in the Army of the Potomac fought at the Battle of Chancellorsville on May 1 through May 4. The Seventh New Jersey Volunteer Infantry captured several hundred prisoners and eight flags in what proved to be ultimately a losing cause. Brigadier General Joseph Warren Revere of Morristown, grandson of Paul Revere, was court-martialed for withdrawing his division from the battle line to refit and rearm without authorization. He was found guilty, but President Lincoln agreed to set aside the verdict if Revere resigned his commission, which he did.

In July, the New Jersey units remaining in the Army of the Potomac (the nine months' service regiments had been discharged) fought in the Battle of Gettysburg. On July 2, Artillery Battery B, deployed near the Peach Orchard, fired 1,342 rounds, more than any other Union artillery battery in the Civil War fired in a single day—and Battery B's day started at 2:00 p.m. On July 3, the men of the Twelfth New Jersey Volunteer Infantry, firing "buck and ball" ammunition in their smoothbore muskets, helped wreck Pickett's Charge on Cemetery Ridge and captured the flag of the Twenty-sixth North Carolina Infantry Regiment.

Former governor Charles S. Olden was elected president of the Loyal National League of New Jersey, an organization that supported the Union effort in the Civil War.

A cranberry craze swept Ocean County and led to a rapid boom in cranberry production that dropped the price of cranberries drastically, ending the boom with a bust.

# 1864

On May 10, the first military draft in New Jersey under the Enrollment Act of 1863 took place in Ocean County, followed a week later by a drawing in Elizabeth. It went off quietly, as local government officials had pledged to pay the $300 "commutation fee" to exempt anyone who did not want to serve. In the end, only 951 men drafted in New Jersey in 1864 and 1865 actually served in the army. The rest either paid commutation or provided a substitute.

On May 12, after heavy fighting in the Wilderness, the First New Jersey Brigade attacked the "Bloody Angle" at Spotsylvania, Virginia, suffering heavy losses. Once told he was too short to be in the army, English-born John P. Beach, of Trenton and the Fourth New Jersey Volunteer Infantry, received the Medal of Honor for his bravery in the attack, although the medal was not awarded until 1894. The brigade continued to fight in the Overland Campaign, the Shenandoah Valley and the siege of Petersburg.

On June 1, Solomon Andrews, former mayor of Perth Amboy, physician and prolific inventor, flew his *Aereon* airship over Perth Amboy. Composed of gasbags and a rudder, the ship, unlike contemporary balloons, was, according to Andrews, navigable through the air—a true "flying machine." Andrews was ahead of his time, but nothing ever materialized from his project.

On July 9, the Fourteenth New Jersey Volunteer Infantry was part of a force that fought a delaying action against Confederate general Jubal Early's raid into Maryland, saving Washington, D.C., from possible capture.

On July 26, James Richard Nugent was born in Newark. Nugent, a graduate of Seton Hall College, became an attorney and leader of the Essex County Democratic Party. His characterization of Woodrow Wilson as a "liar and an ingrate" in 1911 cost him his leadership position.

New Jersey soldiers of the Thirteenth, Thirty-third and Thirty-fifth Volunteer Infantry Regiments fought in Major General William Tecumseh Sherman's Atlanta campaign and the subsequent March to the Sea.

The state gave land grant funds from the Federal government to Rutgers College to establish the College of Agriculture and Mechanics, known at the time as the Scientific School.

In the presidential election of 1864, the Democratic Party candidate, General George B. McClellan, a New Jersey resident, took all 7 of the state's electoral votes. McClellan received 68,020 popular votes in New Jersey, as opposed to 60,724 cast for Lincoln.

## 1865

In January, Colonel Joseph Karge's Second New Jersey Cavalry Regiment returned to Memphis, Tennessee, after a successful raid on Confederate forces at Egypt Station, Mississippi.

On February 1, New Jersey governor Joel Parker presented New Brunswick native Captain Charles Stewart Boggs with a presentation sword in recognition of Boggs's heroic actions in the naval battle leading to the capture of New Orleans in 1862.

On February 2, a "people's convention" of citizens opposed to the monopoly the state granted to the Camden and Amboy Railroad met in Trenton.

On April 2, New Jersey soldiers of the First and Second Brigades were part of General Ulysses S. Grant's breakthrough of the Confederate lines at Petersburg, forcing General Robert E. Lee's Army of Northern Virginia to retreat west to Appomattox, where Lee surrendered on April 9, effectively ending the Civil War.

On July 11, the Second New Jersey Volunteer Infantry of the First New Jersey Brigade, one of the few units of brigade size to maintain exclusive state identification throughout the Civil War, was the last regiment of the brigade mustered out of service. The brigade ranked fourth among all Union army brigades in the number of its men killed and mortally wounded during the conflict—900.

Approximately 77,000 Jerseymen served during the Civil War in the regular army, volunteers, militia, navy and marine corps. Total New Jersey fatalities, from combat, disease, in POW camps and by accidents and unknown causes, totaled 5,754.

## 1866

The New Jersey State Board of Education was established.

The State Home for Disabled Soldiers was founded in Newark.

The United States Blasting Oil Company built a high-explosives factory in Little Ferry. "Blasting oil" was a compound of gunpowder and nitroglycerine and very unstable.

The year proved to be the peak year for freight movement on the Morris Canal, as 459,775 tons of coal and 290,165 tons of iron ore, in addition to significant amounts of "beer, bricks, lumber, lime, grain and manure" traveled over the waterway.

## 1867

On February 12, the Lincoln Association of Jersey City was founded at the Union House. It remains the oldest continuous Lincoln group in the United States.

Michael O'Brian, a native of Cork, Ireland, immigrated to Jersey City before the Civil War. O'Brian served in a New Jersey unit during the war, then returned to Ireland and participated in a jail break that freed Irish rebel prisoners and resulted in the death of a British policeman. O'Brian was captured, tried, sentenced to death and hanged on November 23. One of the freed rebels, Tom Kelly, fled to America, where he and his wife opened a hotel in Atlantic City.

The New Jersey Women Suffrage Association was formed in November, with Lucy Stone as its first president.

Drew Theological Seminary opened in Madison. The school became a liberal arts college in 1928 and a university in 1955.

## 1868

The Porpoise Fishing Company was founded on Pond Creek in Cape May County to make leather from dolphin skins, oil from their fat and steaks from their flesh.

## 1869

On January 1, the Camden and Amboy Railroad's legislatively granted monopoly on transportation across New Jersey between Philadelphia and New York formally expired. Legal challenges and legislative lobbying activity on the part of the railroad hindered its effective end for another seven years, however.

The State of New Jersey combined the New Jersey Rifle Corps, established as an elite militia formation in 1864, and the New Jersey regular uniformed militia into a new part-time state military force called the New Jersey National Guard.

A fire in Cape May destroyed a quarter of the town's business section.

Joseph Campbell and Abram A. Anderson opened a canning plant to pack peas and tomatoes in Camden.

The first intercollegiate football game, between Rutgers and Princeton, took place on November 6. Rutgers won, six to four.

# 1870

The census reported New Jersey's population at 906,096.

The United States Blasting Oil factory in Little Ferry exploded, leaving behind nothing but one chimney.

The New Jersey Railroad, a division of the Pennsylvania Railroad, opened a new bridge over the Passaic River, cutting the travel distance between Newark and Harrison to Jersey City.

On March 31, Thomas Mundy Peterson of Perth Amboy voted in a local election, becoming the first African American to vote under the auspices of the Fifteenth Amendment, ratified the day before.

The first shore resort formal boardwalk, called "Boardman's Walk" after its builder, Alex Boardman, was opened in Atlantic City. Some other resorts dispute Atlantic City's claim, although their initial "boardwalks" were simply boards placed on the sand.

Stevens Institute of Technology was established at Hoboken. It was the first American college to specialize in mechanical engineering.

The National Guard's Sixth Regiment was called out to maintain order as a result of election riots in the town of Centreville, in Camden County.

In December, a feud between the Erie Railroad and the Morris and Essex Railroad over rights of way through the Bergen Tunnel resulted in a Morris and Essex crew placing a "frog" (a section of track acting as a switch) on the tracks to block the Erie and "nearly precipitated a general riot" among employees of both companies, police, passengers and local "idlers." Thousands of people gathered, stalled trains stretched out across the Meadowlands and sporadic fighting broke out. After Governor Theodore F. Randolph appeared on the scene and alerted the National Guard for possible deployment, the matter was finally resolved.

# 1871

Jersey City Irish Americans made no secret of their intent to break up a July parade of Orangemen on the anniversary of the Battle of the Boyne, a 1690 encounter that ensured the Protestant Ascendency in Ireland.

Governor Randolph criticized the Orangemen for starting an "unnecessary" political and religious feud and at the same time guaranteed their right to parade, threatening to call out the National Guard if there were disturbances. There were none.

The Republican-dominated legislature gerrymandered election districts to ensure its own party's dominance for the next two decades. The most egregious new district was "the Horseshoe" in Jersey City, where the Irish neighborhoods were crammed into a single horseshoe-shaped district to lessen the power of their votes.

The Giant Powder Company established a dynamite plant in Kenvil.

Legislation was passed giving women equal rights to child custody in a divorce.

The first African American Masonic lodge was founded in New Jersey.

A statewide free public school system was established.

New York manufacturer James A. Bradley founded the seaside resort of Asbury Park, named after Methodist bishop Francis Asbury.

The Lehigh Valley Railroad purchased the Morris Canal, chiefly to gain its Hudson River waterfront property in Jersey City.

Ellis Parker was born on September 12 in Burlington. As a Burlington County detective, Parker gained wide renown as a sleuth, especially in solving murder cases.

Novelist Stephen Crane was born on November 1 at 14 Mulberry Place in Newark.

# 1872

On the evening of August 20, to the tunes of Reinhard's brass band, the Newark Industrial Exhibition opened to the public in a roller-skating rink expanded to fifty thousand square feet of exhibit space with exhibits by nearly one thousand Newark manufacturers. The Episcopal bishop of New Jersey called the exhibition, which entertained 130,000 visitors during its fifty-five-day run, an "element of perfection where the brazen padlocks glittered like gold; the huge shears were ornamented as if for special beauty; the carriages and harness as though they might have been made for a perpetual showcase." Among the visitors were presidential candidates Horace Greeley and Ulysses S. Grant. "Newark has done well," said Grant. It did well by Grant in the election also, giving him the majority of its votes.

Medical school dropout George G. Green returned to his hometown of Woodbury to take over his father's patent medicine business. Green promoted and marketed his chief products, "Green's August Flower" and "Boschee's German Syrup," by mailing out millions of sample doses and promotional almanacs. It was due to Green's advertising campaign that the small Woodbury Post Office secured seventh place in mail volume and postal revenues in the state. Green's "patent medicine" business made him a fortune, but the passage of the Pure Food and Drug Act of 1906, restricting extravagant claims about patent medicine efficacy, sent his business into decline. He died in Woodbury in 1925.

Political cartoonist Thomas Nast moved from New York City to Morristown.

## 1873

On September 18, also known as "Black Thursday," the investment bank of financier Jay Cooke failed due to bad investments in railroad stocks, setting off the Panic of 1873, a series of big bank failures coupled with railroad bankruptcies. Unemployment soared, and wages plummeted, creating a vortex of downward mobility for many Americans. The downturn lasted six years and hit Jersey City particularly hard.

The first hotel was opened in Asbury Park.

The Singer sewing machine factory opened in Elizabeth.

Walt Whitman moved to Camden. Whitman, perhaps America's greatest poet, would spend the rest of his life in the city on the Delaware.

Civil War veteran Alexander D. Hamilton, treasurer of Jersey City, absconded with much of the treasury and a New York City actress. A detective trailed him to Texas but gave up the chase when Hamilton came under the protection of Mexican politician and sometime bandit Juan Cortina. Cortina subsequently confiscated Hamilton's treasure and put him on a boat to Brazil. Several months later, "the defaulter" made his way back to Jersey City and surrendered.

Cyrus Fogg Brackett became chairman of the Physics Department at Princeton. Brackett later founded the university's Electrical Engineering Department. A friend of both Thomas Edison and Alexander Graham Bell, he is also credited with having the first classroom in America featuring electric lighting.

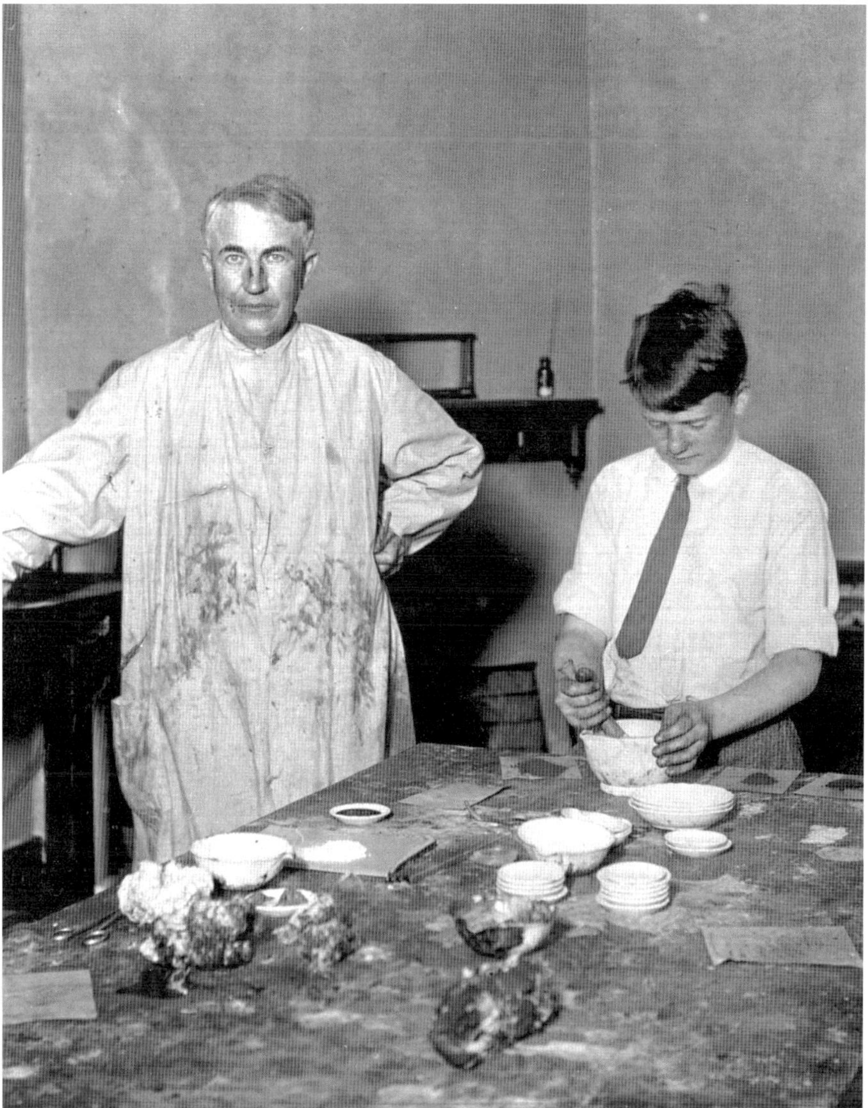

Thomas A. Edison in his West Orange Laboratories with his son Charles, a future governor of New Jersey. *Thomas Edison National Historical Park.*

## 1874

The United States army established its first proving ground to test weapons and ammunition at Sandy Hook.

Seaside Park was founded as a Baptist religious resort.

## 1875

Maine native John F. Dryden founded the Prudential Friendly Society, selling life insurance policies to working-class customers in Newark. The company eventually became the Prudential Insurance Company, and Dryden became very wealthy. He served as a U.S. senator from New Jersey between 1902 and 1907.

Prentice Oil Company established the first oil refinery in Bayonne.

On March 19, Charles K. Landis, founder of Vineland, walked into the offices of the *Vineland Independent* newspaper and shot the editor, Uri Carruth, in the head, killing him. Landis was angry at Carruth, whom he believed had libeled him and his wife in the pages of the paper. He was tried and acquitted on the grounds of "temporary insanity."

## 1876

On August 24, Abraham Browning of Camden, speaking at "Jersey Day" at the Centennial Exhibition in Philadelphia, allegedly first used the term the "Garden State" in reference to New Jersey. Other sources, however, attribute the nickname to an earlier reference to the state seal, with its three plows and figure of Ceres, goddess of agriculture.

Thomas Alva Edison built a laboratory at Menlo Park. It was the world's first industrial research facility, dedicated to applied science and technology.

The New Jersey State Lunatic Asylum at Morristown opened. In 1893, the institution was renamed the Morris Plains Hospital for the Insane and, in 1924, Graystone Park.

# 1877

On February 11, Mabel Smith Douglass, educator, founder and first dean of the New Jersey College for Women (later Douglass College), was born.

On July 14, as the nation remained mired in the depressed economy produced by the Panic of 1873, layoffs and wage cuts became more and more damaging to workers across the economic spectrum. The trouble ignited a great railroad strike that began in West Virginia and spread across the country. National Guard troops called out in West Virginia refused to fire on the strikers, while Maryland guardsmen engaged in pitched battles with them in Baltimore. The Pennsylvania state military killed more than forty demonstrators in Pittsburgh, and federal troops were sent in to end the violence. The conflict spread right up to the border of New Jersey, and New Jersey governor Joseph D. Bedle called up the National Guard in anticipation of violence, but none materialized. Although there were a few minor disturbances, most New Jersey railroad workmen were apparently content with having their grievances heard by management and the public.

Thomas Alva Edison developed the first "talking machine" or phonograph in his Menlo Park laboratory. Edison soon gained the nickname of the "Wizard of Menlo Park."

# 1878

On June 6, John P. Holland of Paterson tested his first submarine design in the Passaic River. Although he claimed it seaworthy, the U.S. Navy rejected his plans.

On August 29, former major general Hugh Judson Kilpatrick held a "First Reunion" of New Jersey Civil War veterans at his farm in Deckertown as a kickoff for his run for a congressional seat. The highlight of the day was a battle reenactment featuring veterans and National Guard soldiers fueled by ten thousand barrels of beer. The event, which also featured food stalls and games of chance, drew four thousand veterans and forty thousand spectators to rural Sussex County. Kilpatrick failed in his election efforts but gained an ambassadorship to Chile, where he died of chronic nephritis on December 2, 1881.

Classes began at Saint Peter's College in Jersey City.

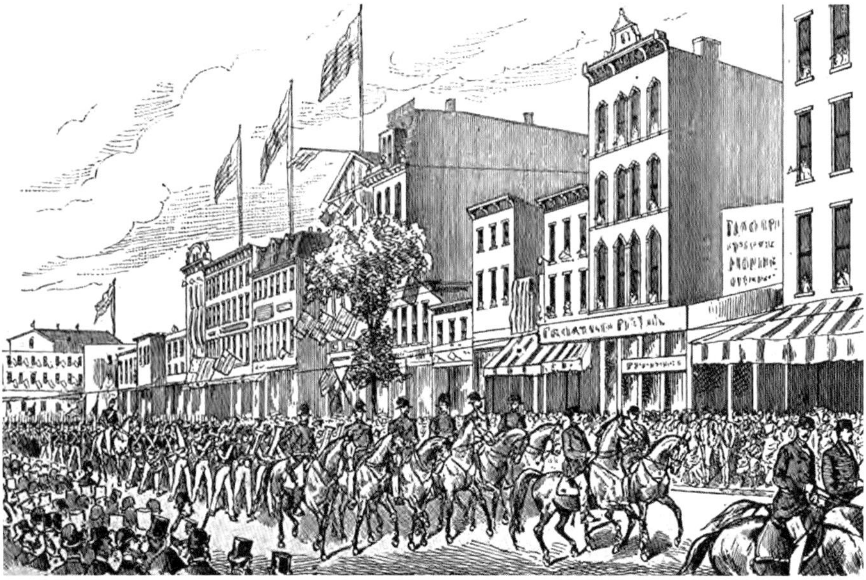

The 1879 parade in Jersey City commemorated the centennial of the Battle of Paulus Hook. *James M. Madden.*

# 1879

On August 19, a parade and memorial ceremony commemorating the centennial celebration of the Battle of Paulus Hook was held in Jersey City.

On November 4, Thomas Alva Edison filed an application for a patent on the "electric lamp" or incandescent bulb.

Ocean City, a resort town in Cape May County, was founded by three Methodist ministers as a liquor-free vacation haven along the lines of Monmouth County's Ocean Grove.

Bay Head was founded by investors from Princeton and soon became a fashionable shore resort, with streets named for Princeton University presidents and professors.

New Yorkers bought seventeen thousand acres of land from the Bricksburg Land & Improvement Company and named their new town Lakewood, promoting it as a winter health resort in the Pinelands.

# 1880

The census reported New Jersey's population as 1,131,116.

Lammot du Pont of the famed Delaware gunpowder-making family bought a farm in Gibbstown and built the largest dynamite plant in the world, the Repauno Dynamite Company.

Railroads held enormous economic and political power in late nineteenth-century New Jersey. In the gubernatorial election of 1880, for example, Democrat George C. Ludlow of Middlesex County ran against Republican Frederick A. Potts of Hunterdon County. Ludlow was an attorney for the Pennsylvania Railroad and Potts a major stockholder in the Jersey Central Railroad. Ludlow won by 651 votes.

The record snowfall for a single month in New Jersey history, 50.1 inches, was reported in Freehold, Monmouth County, in December.

# 1881

On September 19, President James A. Garfield died in Elberon as the result of faulty medical treatment of a gunshot wound inflicted by assassin Charles Guiteau at a Washington train station on July 2.

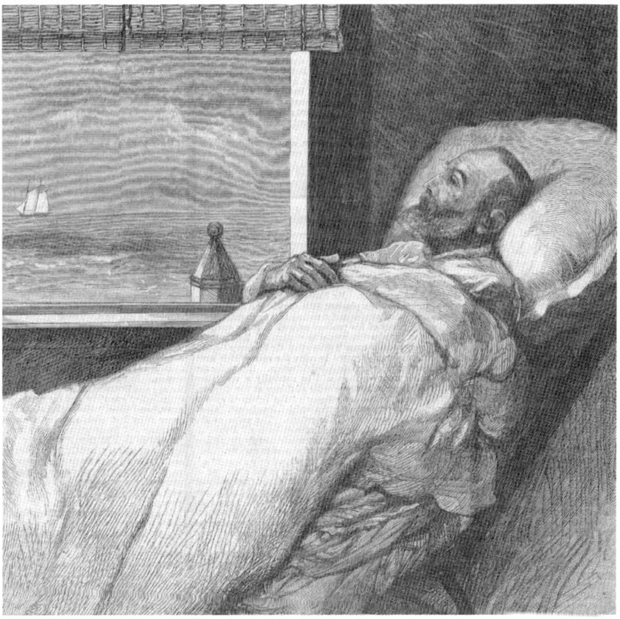

President James A. Garfield in his last days at Elberon. *Joseph G. Bilby.*

James Lafferty Jr. built a six-story wooden elephant in Egg Harbor Township (today's Margate) to attract tourists to the seaside town. Lafferty took out a patent on "Lucy the Elephant" that stated, "My invention consists of a building in the form of an animal." He built two other elephants in other resorts, but Lucy is the only one that survives today.

The Woodbury Glass Works was established. Most of its production went to supply bottles for George G. Green's patent medicine business.

Thomas Alva Edison established an "incandescent lamp" (light bulb) factory in Harrison.

John P. Holland launched an improved submarine, the *Fenian Ram*, in the Hudson River.

## 1882

William F. Halsey Jr., who graduated from the U.S. Naval Academy in 1904 and rose to become commander of the U.S. Third Fleet in the Pacific in World War II, was born in Elizabeth on October 30.

Eleven cases of smallpox were reported in Hoboken.

## 1883

The first electric lighting system featuring overhead wires was installed in Roselle by Thomas Edison's company.

On January 20, Enoch L. "Nucky" Johnson, future Republican political boss of Atlantic County and sometime gangster who was the inspiration for the fictional "Nucky Thompson" of the HBO series *Boardwalk Empire*, was born in Galloway Township.

Up to 103 trains a day were stopping at the Ocean Grove/Asbury Park station in the summer, as the Jersey shore boomed in the post–Civil War era.

Leon Abbett was elected governor of New Jersey for the first time. Born in 1836 to a poor working-class family in Philadelphia, Abbett rose to become a prominent attorney but was considered a man of the people and known to his supporters as the "Great Commoner." Abbett, who served two nonconsecutive terms as governor, not only championed workers but was

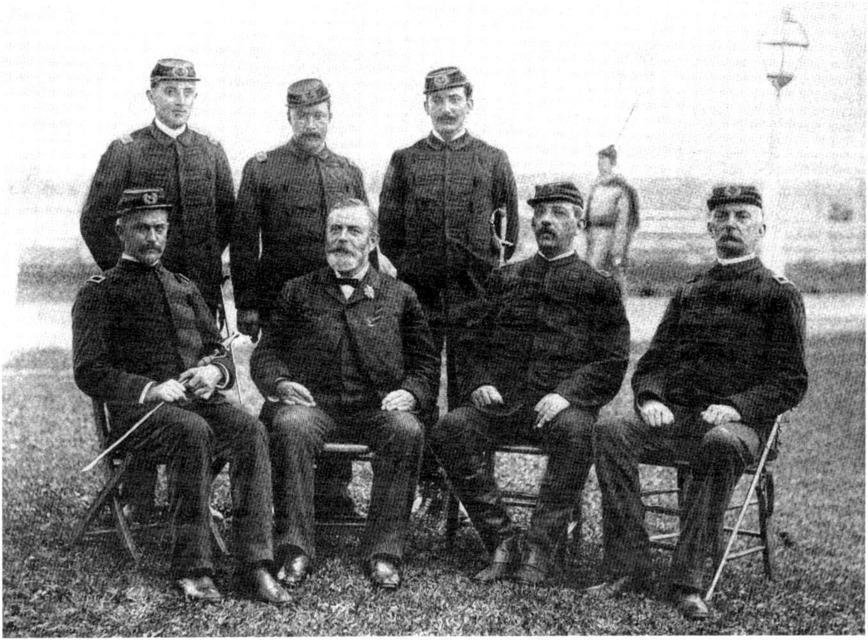

Governor Leon Abbett (seated, second from left) at Sea Girt. *NGMMNJ.*

also a sophisticated politician who created an effective political machine in Hudson County.

## 1884

On January 26, the parishioners of Hackensack's mixed-race First Baptist Church were advised by the Hackensack Cemetery Company that they could not bury their deceased sexton, Samuel Bass, an African American, in the cemetery because it was a "whites only" burial ground and he was an "objectionable person." The church's white minister described the decision as "bigoted, unchristianlike and contrary to the spirit of our institutions." Governor Abbett strongly condemned the cemetery company's racism and pushed hard for a political remedy. The result was the passage of the "Negro Burial Bill," which outlawed discrimination by cemeteries.

Lammot du Pont was killed in an explosion at his dynamite factory on March 29.

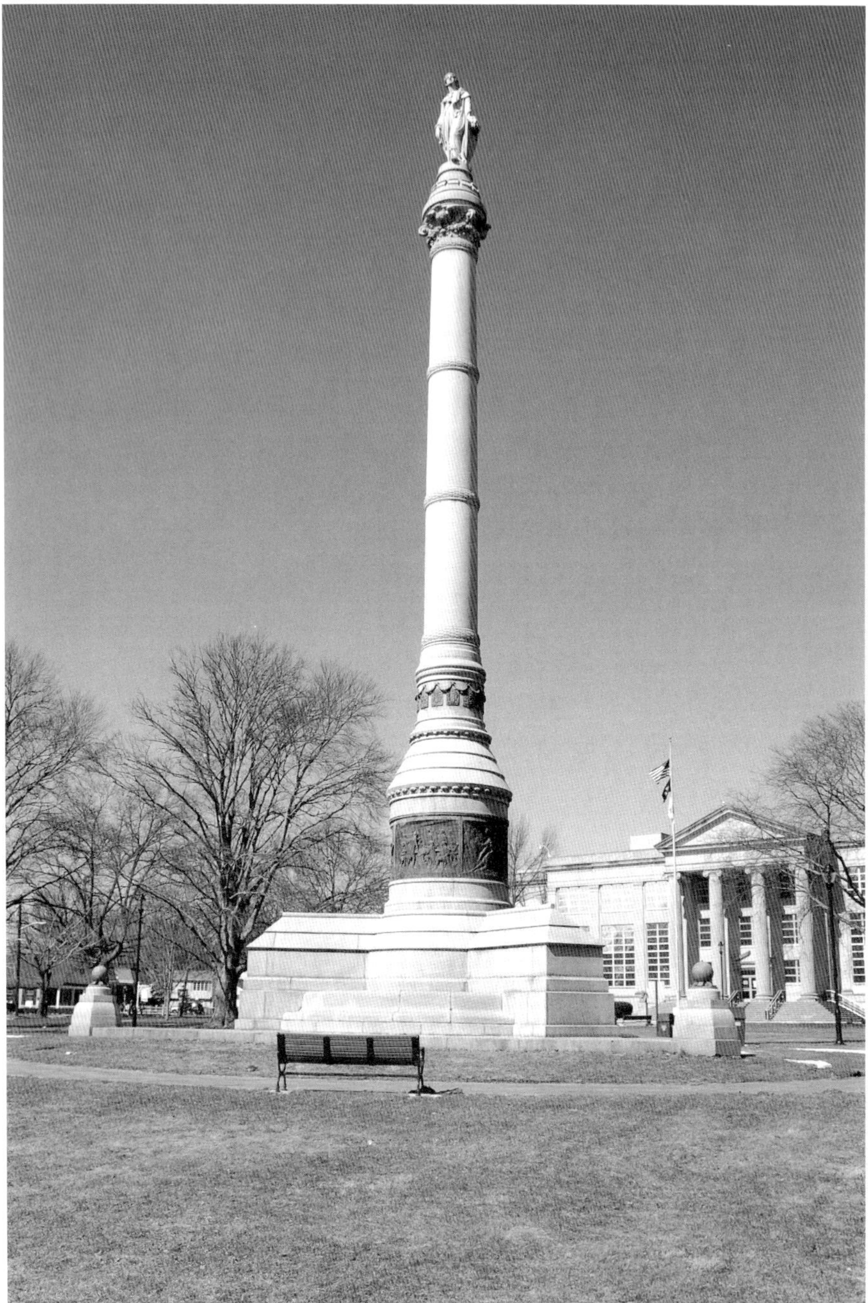

Battle of Monmouth monument erected in 1884. *Joseph G. Bilby.*

A monument to the 1778 Battle of Monmouth Courthouse was officially unveiled in Freehold on November 13. New York sculptor James E. Kelly created the relief sculptures of events from the campaign on the monument base, and his friend Thomas Edison served as a model for an artilleryman in Kelly's portrayal of Molly Pitcher. The statue atop the monument, *Columbia Triumphant*, was struck by lightning and seriously damaged in 1894 and replaced in 1896.

The New Jersey National Guard leased property in Manasquan for its annual field training. The shore provided an excellent venue for long-range target shooting, which was popular at the time among both military and civilian shooters.

## 1885

Alice Stokes Paul, social reformer and champion of women's suffrage, was born near Moorestown on January 11.

On March 21, the statehouse in Trenton was partially destroyed by a fire.

Standard Oil of New Jersey was incorporated.

Robert W. and James W. Johnson formed a company in New Brunswick to produce gauze and adhesive tape. Production began the following year, and from those beginnings, the company developed into a world-famous medical device and pharmaceutical firm.

The New Jersey National Guard held its annual training in Sea Girt for the first time. The state leased, and then later purchased, the Sea Girt property, which it retains to this day. Governor Abbett visited the camp to review the troops, setting a precedent that would lead New Jersey's governors to spend much of the summer at Sea Girt in succeeding years.

## 1886

On May 26, the Gettysburg monument to the Twelfth New Jersey Volunteer Infantry was dedicated on Cemetery Ridge. The monument was the first New Jersey monument erected at Gettysburg and was privately funded by veterans of the regiment.

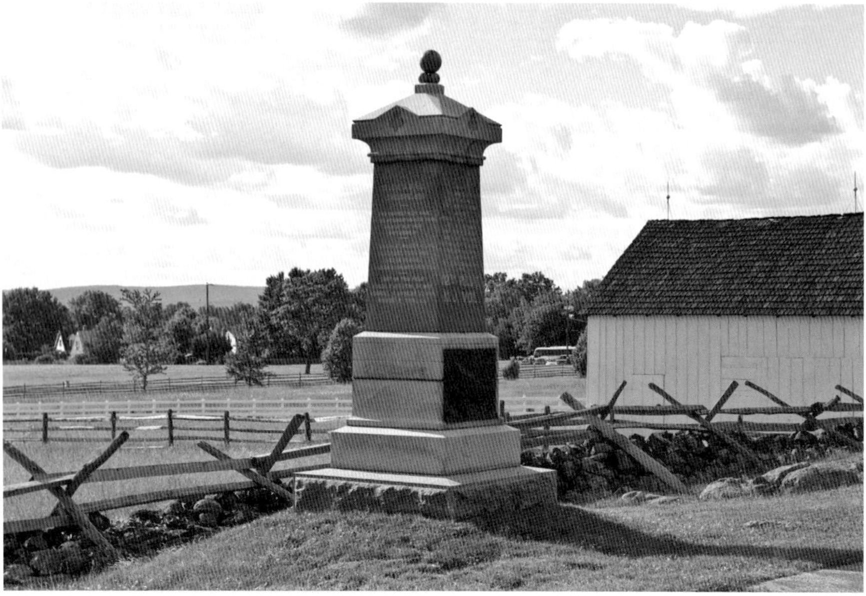

The Twelfth New Jersey Infantry's monument on Cemetery Ridge at Gettysburg. *Henry Ballone.*

Alfred Joyce Kilmer, journalist, poet and World War I soldier, was born on December 6 in New Brunswick. Kilmer was serving as a sergeant with the 165th Infantry Regiment (the famed 69th New York Irish-American National Guard unit) when he was killed in action on July 30, 1918.

## 1887

Thomas Alva Edison opened his new laboratory in West Orange on November 24.

Newark minister Reverend Hannibal Goodwin invented flexible nitrocellulose film.

A debate in the New Jersey Assembly over whom to elect as a U.S. senator (senators were elected by state legislatures until 1913) led to "fist shaking… ribald language and a physical fight over the Speaker's gavel."

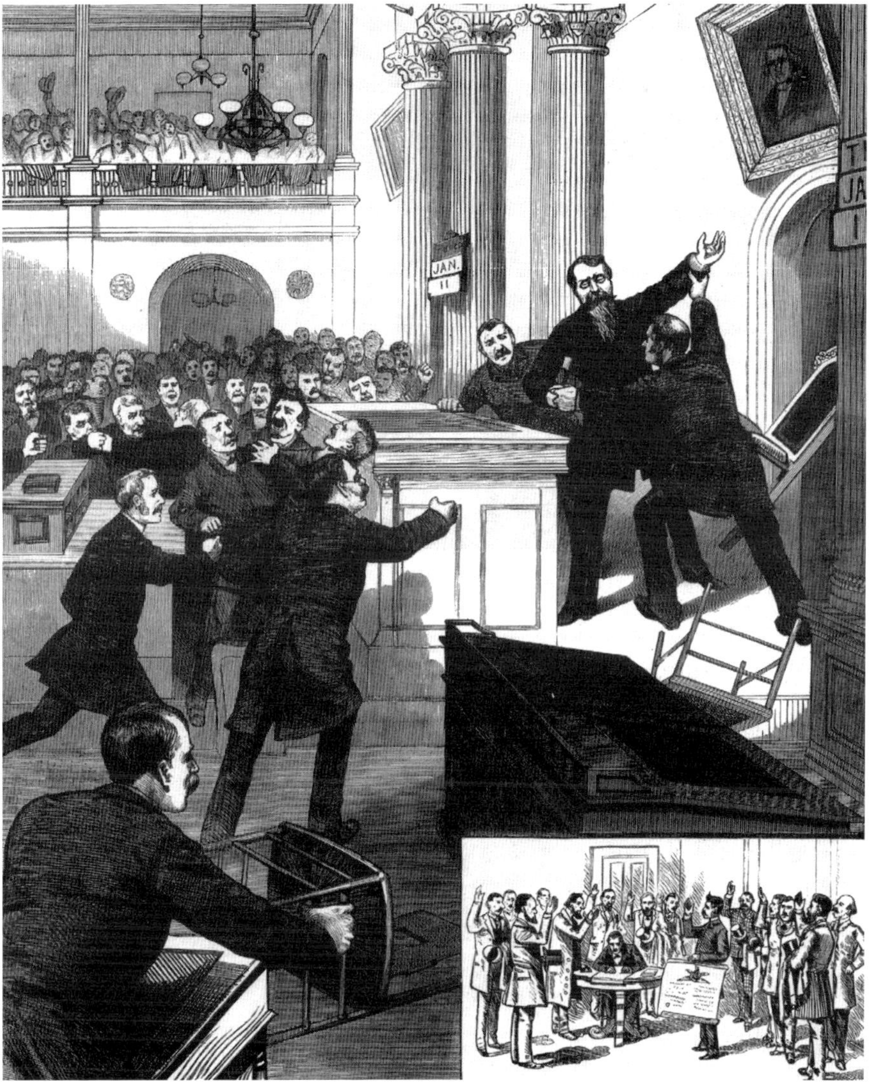


New Jersey assemblymen engaged in a brawl over possession of the assembly gavel in 1887. *James M. Madden.*

# 1888

On June 30, "New Jersey Day," at Gettysburg Battlefield, Governor Robert S. Green led an official delegation that formally dedicated most of the monuments erected on the field by the state to honor the New Jersey soldiers who fought there.

President Benjamin Harrison awarded Joseph Francis of Toms River the Congressional Gold Medal, designed by Augustus Saint-Gaudens, for his invention of the life-car used to rescue people from in-shore shipwrecks.

## 1889

On April 24, the first electric trolley in New Jersey began its run in Atlantic City.

A hurricane that proved to be one of New Jersey's worst and most destructive storms hit the coast on September 8 and stalled through September 12, submerging many of the barrier islands.

A rebuilt statehouse, with a new dome and wing designed by Jersey City architect Louis Broome, opened in Trenton. Additions were constructed in 1891 and 1903.

Samuel Leeds Allen of Cinnaminson Township was granted a patent on the "flexible flier" sled.

Blacksmith John Bell of Park Ridge claimed his house was cursed by "the diabolic influence of witches" and that they, among other things, made knives and forks dance on his kitchen table and "an empty pair of trousers" walk down a flight of stairs "behind its owner."

## 1890

The census reported New Jersey's population as 1,444,933.

On May 14, a statue of inventor Seth Boyden was unveiled in Newark's Washington Park by Mayor Joseph Haynes. The "Essex Club," a gentlemen's riding club that provided an escort for the mayor that day, later joined the National Guard as the "Essex Troop," which eventually became the core unit of the 102nd Cavalry, a military organization still active in the state's National Guard.

Philip Pontius Baker, a state senator from Cumberland County who lived in Vineland, founded the resort town of Wildwood on Five Mile Beach.

Princeton graduate Woodrow Wilson, class of 1879, returned to the university as a professor.

Thomas Alva Edison established Edison General Electric Company.

Construction began on a new modern fort at Sandy Hook, which was intended to be the first line of defense for New York City. It would grow into Fort Hancock.

The United States government established an immigrant processing station on Ellis Island, gaining title, but not sovereignty, from New York. That sovereignty was long disputed by New Jersey. The station remained in operation until 1954.

## 1891

On January 18, Captain John McGowan, who sailed the *Star of the West* into Charleston Harbor in 1861 and became a target for South Carolina gunners, died at his home in Elizabeth. He was buried in Evergreen Cemetery in Hillside.

On May 20, Thomas Edison demonstrated a prototype of his kinetoscope short film viewing machine to members of the National Federation of Women's Clubs at his West Orange laboratory.

John Blake, owner of the Pole Tavern in Gloucester, killed his 1,157-pound hog at the conclusion of a weight-guessing contest that drew attention from all over southern New Jersey.

Thomas Robins built the first rubber belt conveyor to carry ore at Thomas Edison's Ogden Mine in Sussex County. Robins later founded a conveyor belt manufacturing company in Passaic. His invention won him a Grand Prize at the Paris Exposition of 1900.

The New Jersey chapter of the Good Roads movement, formed by bicyclists, successfully lobbied state government to pass the first state aid for roadway construction in the country.

## 1892

Swedesboro was the site of the first mile of stone road in New Jersey.

Walt Whitman, the "good gray poet," died in Camden on March 26 and was buried in Camden's Harleigh Cemetery in a self-designed mausoleum. His home in Camden is a state historic site, and he is otherwise commemorated in typical New Jersey style, with a bridge and a turnpike rest area in his name.

On July 9, a five-hundred-pound shell fired from the ordnance testing range at Sandy Hook accidentally hit the schooner *Henry R. Tilton* and sank it.

Otto James Messmer, creator of the cartoon character Felix the Cat, was born on August 16 in West Hoboken (today's Union City).

On September 26, John Philip Sousa's band performed for the first time in public at the Stillman Music Hall in Plainfield.

The "Bicycle Railway," a passenger-powered monorail connecting Smithville and Mount Holly, designed by Arthur Hotchkiss, began operation. It lasted until 1898.

Edison General Electric merged with the Thomson-Houston Electric Company to form General Electric.

Louis Bamberger, Louis Frank and Felix Fuld established Bamberger's Department Store, an iconic part of the Newark shopping scene for a century.

## 1893

Famed markswoman and *Buffalo Bill Wild West Show* entertainer Annie Oakley and her husband, Frank Butler, moved to Nutley, New Jersey.

The Black Maria, the world's first motion picture studio, was built at the Thomas Alva Edison laboratories in West Orange.

## 1894

On January 4, an experimental kinetoscope film of Thomas Edison's employee Fred Ott sneezing was filmed at the Edison Laboratories in West Orange. It was the first motion picture copyrighted in the United States.

J. Noah H. Slee developed Three-in-One Oil in a shack in Rahway and began to sell it to the public.

Jersey City resident Mary Philbrook's application to take the New Jersey bar examination was rejected because "there was no enabling legislation allowing women to practice law in the state."

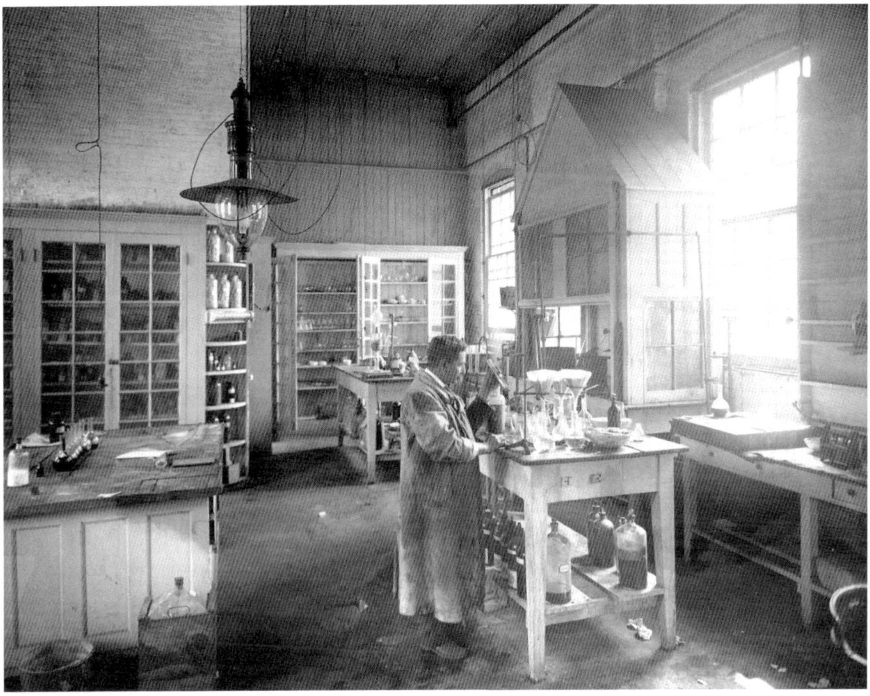

Fred Ott, famous for his role in *The Sneeze* film, at work in the Edison Laboratory in West Orange at the turn of the twentieth century. *Thomas Edison National Historical Park.*

A group of women in Morristown founded the Morris County Golf Club, the first country club in the United States run by women. Within two years, men had wrested control of the club from them.

Thomas Edison filmed a marksmanship demonstration by Annie Oakley in his Black Maria film studio in West Orange. Where the bullets ended up after passing through Maria's thin skin is unknown.

## 1895

In June, after enabling legislation was passed by the state legislature, Mary Philbrook passed her bar examination and became the first female attorney to practice in New Jersey. She devoted her legal career to public service and equal rights for women.

On July 13, a tornado hit Bergen County, destroying most of the houses in the little town of Cherry Hill near Hackensack. Three people were killed, and another eleven injured. The tornado then passed over the Palisades and Harlem and touched ground again at Woodhaven, Long Island, where it killed another person.

The Essex County Park Commission was established to preserve the county's parks, including, at that time, Eagle Rock, South Mountain, Branch Brook and Weequahic.

The new fort at Sandy Hook, still under construction, was formally named Fort Hancock.

## 1896

Two trains collided at a crossing just west of Atlantic City on July 30, smashing five passenger coaches. Fifty people were killed and over sixty seriously injured.

## 1897

Campbell executive John T. Dorrance introduced the line of condensed soups that made the Camden-based company famous worldwide.

## 1898

Paul Robeson, Rutgers' first all-American football player, as well as class valedictorian, Phi Beta Kappa scholar and later famous actor, singer and political activist, was born in Princeton on April 9.

On April 25, Spain, rejecting American demands for the surrender of Cuba, declared war on the United States.

New Jersey received a request from the federal government to supply three regiments of volunteer infantry through the National Guard structure for two years' service in the Spanish-American War. In early May, National Guardsmen reported to Sea Girt, where volunteers were organized into regiments for the war. The First Regiment was sent to Camp Alger, Virginia, where it was assigned to guard supplies. The Second Regiment was sent to Jacksonville, Florida, and moved from there to Pablo Beach, Florida. One battalion of the

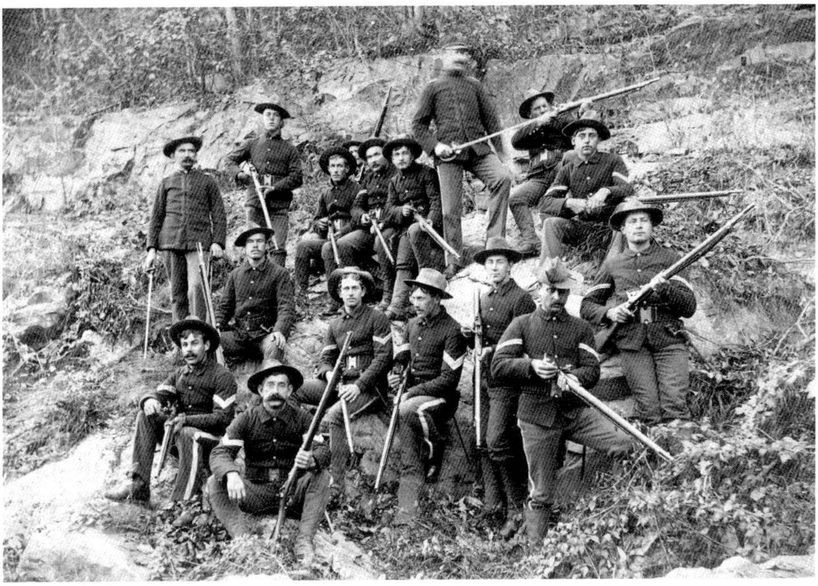

Soldiers of the Third New Jersey Volunteer Regiment at Pompton during the Spanish American War. *NGMMNJ.*

Third Regiment was sent to Pompton Lakes to guard the Laflin and Rand Powder Works, and the regiment's other two battalions were assigned to Fort Hancock on Sandy Hook. In November, the Third moved to Athens, Georgia. A second call produced a Fourth Regiment, which was sent to Camp Meade, Pennsylvania, and then Greenville, South Carolina. No New Jersey regiment ever left the country, and all were discharged by February 1899.

New Jersey's two naval militia battalions were mobilized and assigned to three navy ships: the monitor gunboat USS *Montauk*, which was stationed in Maine during the war, and two "auxiliary vessels," USS *Badger* and USS *Resolute*, both of which were deployed in the blockade of Cuba.

Three New Jerseyans received the Medal of Honor during the Spanish-American War: Sergeant Alexander M. Quinn of Passaic and the Thirteenth U.S. Infantry Regiment and Privates William H. Thompkins and George H. Wanton of Paterson and the African American Tenth U.S. Cavalry Regiment.

On July 12, there was an explosion in Pompton at the "Government mills for the manufacture of smokeless powder." Nine buildings were destroyed and nine workers injured.

On August 12, the Treaty of Paris was signed, ending the Spanish-American War.

## 1899

On April 19, via General Orders No. 5, the New Jersey National Guard was reorganized into four infantry regiments of twelve companies each, two Gatling gun companies, two troops of cavalry and two battalions of the naval militia.

On September 30, Gugielmo Marconi received the first wireless message from a ship at the Twin Lights in Highlands. He went on to establish a transatlantic overseas reception station in Wall Township, at the current location of the Info-Age Museum.

The New York Shipbuilding Company began to build a new shipyard in Camden.

The State Board of Children's Guardians was created to place orphaned children, many of them living in almshouses, in foster homes.

The Sisters of Charity of Saint Elizabeth established the College of Saint Elizabeth in Morristown. It was New Jersey's first four-year liberal arts college for women.

## 1900

The census reported New Jersey's population as 1,883,669.

Gaetano Bresci, an Italian immigrant silk weaver and anarchist from Paterson, purchased a pistol and then left the city and his job and returned to Europe. On July 29, he shot and killed King Umberto of Italy in a village near Milan.

In April, after extensive testing at Sandy Hook, the federal government approved the purchase of Paterson inventor John P. Holland's successful submarine, the *Holland*.

Born on June 28, 1876, in Newark, Clara Louise Maas graduated from the Newark German Hospital School of Nursing and became an army contract nurse during the Spanish-American War. In 1900, while serving in Cuba after the war, Maas volunteered to be bitten by a mosquito in an experiment in the effort to find a cure for yellow fever. She contracted yellow fever and died as a result, and her body was returned to Newark, where she was buried with military honors. In 1918, the Newark German Hospital was renamed Clara Maas Hospital in her memory.

Chapter 6

# 1901 to 1950

## 1901

On September 11, Delaware, Lackawanna and Western Railroad engineer John "Pop" Draney of Jersey City was selected to bring Dr. Janeway, a celebrated New York physician, to Buffalo to attend to President McKinley, who had been shot by an assassin. Draney recalled, "I ran that 395 miles in 405 minutes. We had a green light all the way and I went so fast the doctor rode all the way to Buffalo

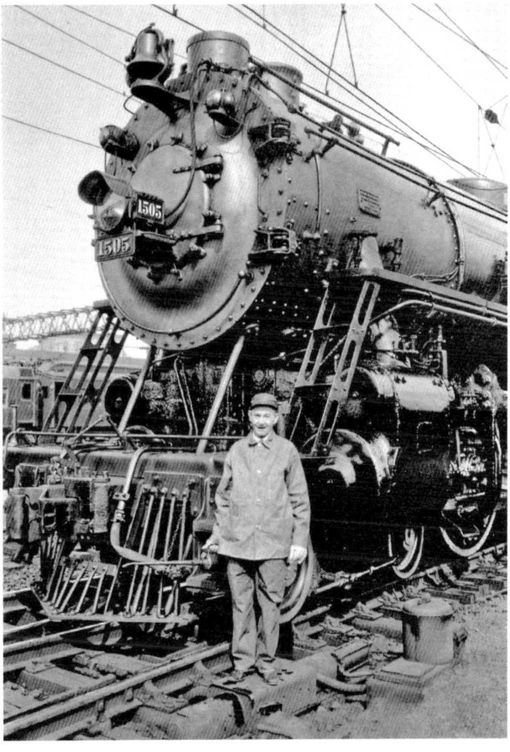

Legendary Delaware Lackawanna and Western Railroad engineer John "Pop" Draney and his engine in 1931. *Carol Fowler/ Michael T. Sullivan.*

sitting in the aisle." Draney retired in 1931 but remained active all his life, appearing as an eighty-nine-year-old panelist on the television show *Life Begins at 80* in 1950.

Eldridge R. Johnson incorporated the Victor Talking Machine Company in Camden. It would evolve into RCA Victor and become the largest producer of phonograph records in the world.

## 1902

Morris "Moe" Berg was born in New York City on March 2. Raised in Newark, Berg was known as the best baseball player that the city had ever produced at the time, and he went on to graduate from Princeton University and Columbia Law School. Berg became a major-league baseball player, World War II Office of Strategic Services (the forerunner of the CIA) agent and legendary eccentric character in the Roseville section of Newark.

Famed New Jersey folklorist Henry Charlton Beck was born in Philadelphia on May 26. From their beginning in the 1930s with *Forgotten Towns of Southern New Jersey*, Beck's books and, later, his newspaper column preserved and popularized New Jersey lore for generations to come. They are still in print.

On July 24, President Theodore Roosevelt visited New Jersey governor Franklin Murphy at the National Guard Camp at Sea Girt and reviewed the guardsmen conducting their annual training there. More than ten thousand people flocked to the little seaside town to see the immensely popular president.

Princeton professor Woodrow Wilson was appointed president of the university.

## 1903

In February, a trolley car full of Newark high school students slid on icy tracks and crashed through a gate across the Delaware Lackawanna and Western Railroad tracks into the path of an oncoming locomotive. Nine of the students were killed. A grand jury indicted the officers of the trolley company, the North Jersey Street Line, for manslaughter, but a trial jury failed to convict. A grand juror later charged that political chicanery and bribery had secured the result, although the assertion was never proven.

In October, a three-day rainfall of 15.04 inches caused the Passaic River to overflow, inundating the city of Paterson.

Townships were authorized to appoint local forest fire wardens.

The "Great Train Robbery," a twelve-minute western-themed motion picture considered the first narrative film, was produced by Thomas Alva Edison and filmed by Edwin S. Porter at various locations in New Jersey, including the tracks of the Delaware, Lackawanna and Western Railroad.

## 1904

The lowest temperature ever officially recorded in New Jersey was noted at River Vale, Bergen County, on January 5. The thermometer measured minus thirty-four degrees Fahrenheit.

Jazz musician, composer and bandleader William "Count" Basie was born on August 21 in Red Bank.

## 1905

Dr. William H. Demarest became president of Rutgers College. The student body totaled 235 at the time.

The town of Roebling was designed and built as a planned industrial community, with housing for the workers within walking distance of the Roebling steel mill. The Roebling family sold the mill to Colorado Fuel and Iron in 1952, and it closed in 1974. As with many New Jersey manufacturing plants hailed in their heyday as exemplars of modernity, the mill location is now a Superfund site.

Muckraking journalist Lincoln Steffens's article "New Jersey: A Traitor State" appeared in the April issue of *McClure's* magazine. Steffens's accusation was based on the effective railroad corporate control of many of New Jersey's leading politicians and legislators, as well as the state's deliberately lax incorporation laws that allowed large trusts to nominally headquarter in New Jersey for tax evasion purposes.

# 1906

Idealistic twenty-eight-year-old writer Upton Sinclair, then living in a "tarpaper shack" in Princeton, completed his novel *The Jungle*, detailing the unsanitary horrors of the slaughterhouse industry. After President Theodore Roosevelt read the book, he called on Congress to pass the Pure Food and Drug Act.

The New Jersey exhibition hall at the 1904 Louisiana Purchase Exposition in Saint Louis, which was modeled on the Ford Mansion in Morristown, was disassembled and brought to Sea Girt, where it was reassembled as the New Jersey governor's summer "cottage" and became popularly known as "the Little White House," the title formerly bestowed on its predecessor, a simple farmhouse. The Little White House was bulldozed in 1971, but the farmhouse still stands.

# 1907

A new state law forbade children under sixteen from working more than fifty-eight hours a week or in retail stores at night.

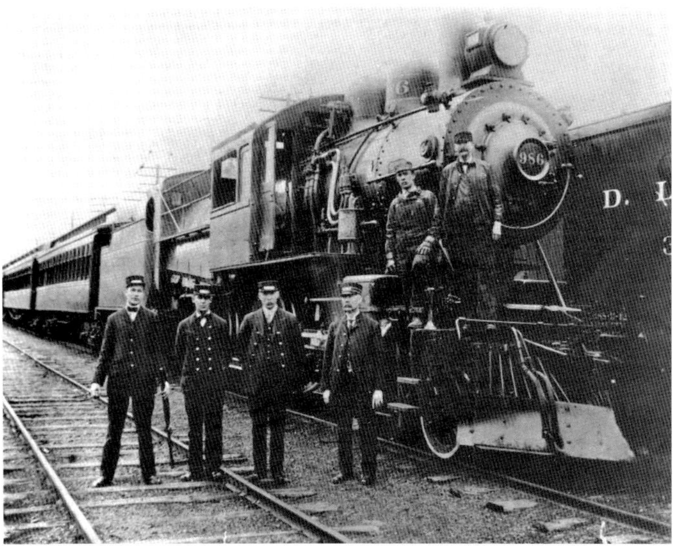

New Jersey was the terminus of many railroads in the late nineteenth century. A Delaware Lackawanna and Western crew photographed in Dover Yards, 1907. The engineer (right) is George H. Bilby, author Joseph Bilby's grandfather. *Joseph G. Bilby.*

# 1908

The first radio broadcast in New Jersey, via an arc transmitting station, was transmitted from Newark. The voices of Mayor Jacob Haussling of Newark and Governor John Franklin Fort went out over the airways.

The name of the Sandy Hook lightship was changed to the Ambrose lightship.

Georgian Court College for women was founded by the Sisters of Mercy in North Plainfield. In 1925, the college moved from North Plainfield to its current home in Lakewood, where the Sisters of Mercy purchased the estate of philandering financier George Jay Gould from his heirs. The campus was named a National Historic Landmark in 1985, and the college became a university in 2004.

The New Jersey State Normal School at Montclair was opened as a two-year teacher training institute. In 1927, it became a four-year school known as Montclair State Teacher's College and became Montclair State College in 1958 and Montclair State University in 1994.

# 1909

The Standard Oil Company opened a pumping station in Linden on January 2.

A Trenton theater doorkeeper, William Cromley, swore that he saw the winged reptile/bird/canine hybrid known as the Jersey Devil on his way home from work, and Claudius P. Weeden, of 217 Brunswick Avenue, testified that the cloven-hoofed beast flew by his window. These stories and more were part of a seeming mass hallucination that spread from Woodbury, New Jersey, to Morrisville, Pennsylvania, between January 16 and January 23. The Jersey Devil, seldom seen prior to this outside his Pineland home, never returned to Trenton, at least not in that form.

Mary Pickford made her film debut at Fort Lee in 1909 when she acted in *The Violin Maker of Cremona.*

# 1910

The census reported New Jersey's population as 2,537,167.

Newark got its first "skyscraper" in the form of the sixteen-story Fireman's Insurance Company building on Broad Street.

Woodrow Wilson, running as a progressive reformer, was elected governor.

Monmouth County sheriff Clarence Hetrick saved Thomas Williams, a black handyman arrested on suspicion of murdering ten-year-old Marie Smith, from lynching by an angry Asbury Park mob. Hetrick himself holstered a handgun to help protect the prisoner. The only post–Revolutionary War New Jersey lynching had occurred in Monmouth County in 1886. Williams was later proved innocent of the charges.

## 1911

Irish-born Robert "Little Bob" Davis, Jersey City alderman, Hudson County sheriff, supervisor of the county jail and Democratic Party political boss, died in Jersey City, making way for the rise of Frank Hague, the most famous New Jersey political boss of all time.

Completion of the Hudson and Manhattan Railroad between Newark and New York greatly accelerated the intermingling of the populations of both cities and hastened Newark's development. The new rapid transit attracted thousands to move from Manhattan to Newark and its suburbs and in turn made going to New York, or "the city," for business or pleasure, a Newark custom.

## 1912

Cartoonist Charles Addams, creator of the *Addams Family* cartoon, was born in Westfield on January 7.

On July 2, the 258-foot semi-rigid airship *Akron*, piloted by its designer, Melvin Vaniman, took off from Atlantic City in an attempt to cross the Atlantic Ocean. As the *Akron* flew over Absecon Beach, it exploded and crashed into the water, killing all five crew members.

The first airmail delivery by fixed-wing aircraft in New Jersey was made from South Amboy to Perth Amboy on July 4 in a hydroplane flown by O.G. Simmonds, who was accompanied by Perth Amboy mayor F. Garretson. Mayor Garretson placed the leather mailbag on his lap, sat on two wooden cross pieces and held onto the plane's struts with both hands.

William Howard Taft, running for reelection as president, called the industrial sprawl across the New Jersey meadowlands in Hudson County

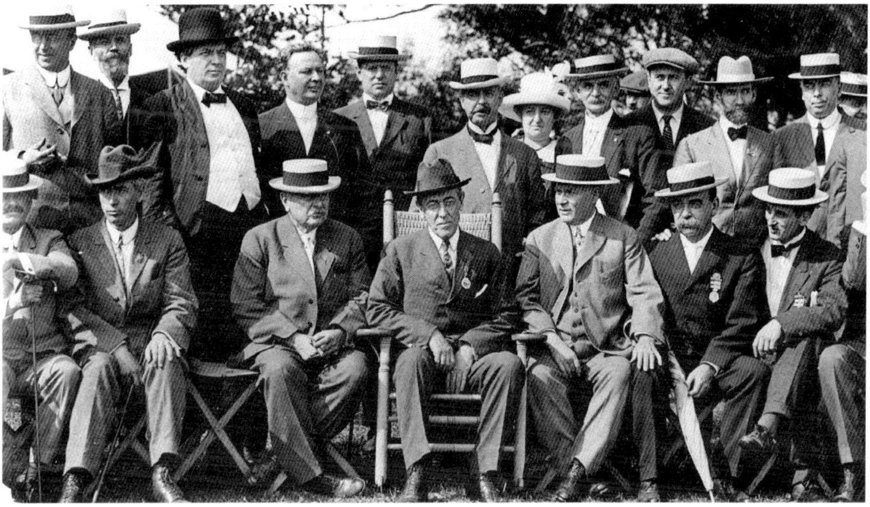

Woodrow Wilson met with Democratic politicians at Sea Girt, 1912. *Joseph G. Bilby.*

a "hive of industry." Later generations, dealing with the residue, were not quite as sanguine.

Woodrow Wilson, governor of New Jersey, received the Democratic Party nomination for president and was elected to that office.

Washington Crossing State Park was established along the Delaware River eight miles north of Trenton, at the site where George Washington landed in his famous crossing of the Delaware in 1776.

## 1913

The great Paterson silk mill strike began with a January 27 walkout of the eight hundred men and women employed by the Henry Doherty Silk Company after workers who attempted to negotiate with management on hours and working conditions were fired. The walkout led to a general strike involving twenty-two thousand workers that lasted twenty-two weeks but, unlike earlier strikes, was marked by nonviolence. The highly publicized support of the artistic and literary community proved to be of not much help, and mill owners simply shifted production to other locations. In the end, the strikers lost their fight for an eight-hour day, but the owners relented on making a weaver run four looms instead of two. Six years later, the workers did gain the eight-hour day.

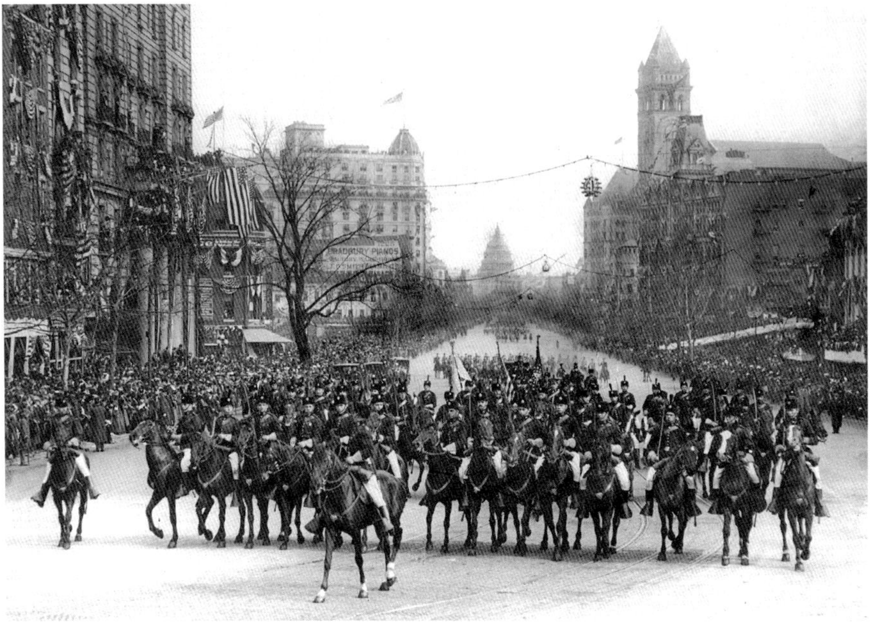

The Essex Troop in President Wilson's inaugural parade. *NGMMNJ.*

On March 4, New Jersey governor Woodrow Wilson was inaugurated as president of the United States. His inaugural parade was highlighted by the appearance of the Essex Troop, a New Jersey National Guard cavalry unit from Newark wearing British-influenced dress uniforms custom tailored by Brooks Brothers in New York City.

On October 13, a statue of Pieter Stuyvesant, sculpted by J. Massey Rhind and dubbed "Peg Leg Pete" by locals, was dedicated at Jersey City's Bergen Square. It was intended to represent the founding of the first permanent settlement in what is now Jersey City.

The world champion oyster shucking competition finals were held in Keyport. The winner shucked five hundred oysters in twenty minutes and twenty-three seconds, for a prize of $300.

## 1914

When World War I broke out in Europe in late July, sympathies in America divided along domestic lines in New Jersey's large first- and second-generation immigrant communities. (An estimated 25 percent of New Jersey's population, according to the 1910 census, was foreign born.) New Jersey's German Americans were joined by many Irish Americans, who expressed their opposition to everything British by sympathizing with Germany and Austria-Hungary, especially after the failed 1916 Easter rising in Dublin.

On August 12, as the conflict that would bring his deadly invention into its own as a weapon of modern war began to rage across Europe, submarine inventor John P. Holland died in Newark.

A fire on December 9 damaged or destroyed thirteen factory buildings at the Edison West Orange laboratories.

Joshua Lionel Cowen, founder of the Lionel Corporation, the world's biggest maker of toy electric trains, moved his operations from New York to Newark. Lionel later moved to Irvington before finally building a factory on the Hillside-Irvington border in 1921, where the company remained until 1970. True to its Jersey roots, the Lionel Corporation used the Beaux-Arts Asbury Park station, built in 1922, as a model for a miniature replica sold with its train sets.

Actress Pearl White filmed literal "cliffhanger" episodes of *The Perils of Pauline* on the Palisades in 1914, in which she hung off the Palisades cliffs overlooking the Hudson River, helping establish the new genre of movie serials.

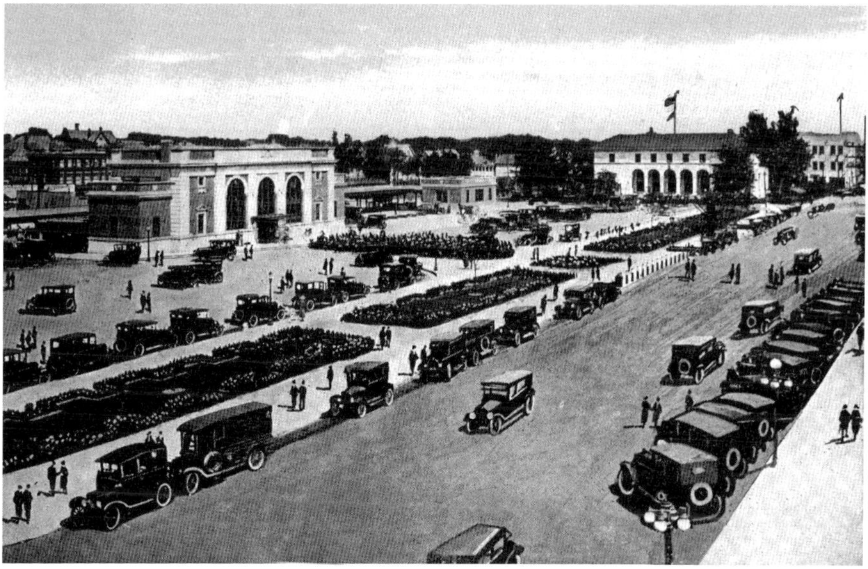

Asbury Park station used as a model by Lionel. *Asbury Park Library.*

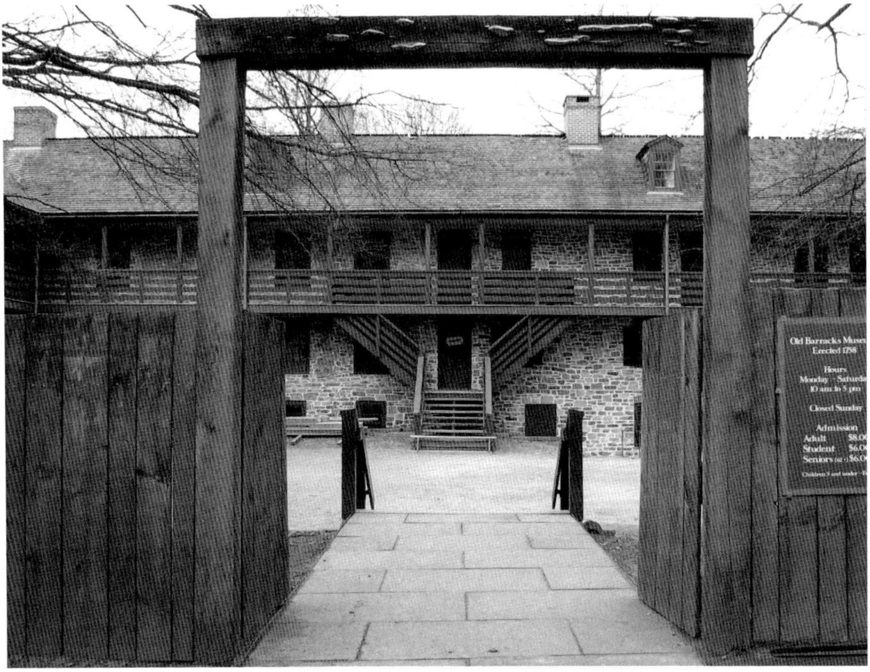

The Old Barracks as it is today. *Geoffrey Jenkins.*

The Old Barracks Association, which had purchased the remains of the French and Indian War barracks in Trenton, deeded the property to the state. In the following two years, the building was restored, and the missing central section, taken down to put a road through many years before, was reconstructed. The Old Barracks Association has run the historic site on behalf of the state ever since.

## 1915

In January, "deputy sheriffs" hired from a Newark detective agency fired on an unarmed group of pickets standing outside the Williams and Clark fertilizer factory in Carteret. Various reports indicated that between one and six strikers were killed and between fifteen and twenty-eight were wounded.

On May 3, an explosion at the Anderson Chemical Plant in Wallington killed three people. Even though the United States was not actively involved in World War I, the allies bought large amounts of ammunition from American makers, and the increase in production resulted in a series of ammunition and chemical plant explosions around the country, many of them in the highly industrialized state of New Jersey.

On October 19, a statewide referendum was held on amending the New Jersey state constitution to allow extending the right to vote to women. The voters were, necessarily, all men. The measure failed by a vote of 184,390 to 133,282.

A series of mysterious fires and an explosion broke out at the John A. Roebling's Sons steel plant in Trenton, damaging the plant and a row of workers' houses. Washington Roebling blamed the fire on "disaffected foreigners" angered by labor issues, but many thought it possible German sabotage. The cause was never conclusively proven.

Local politicians boosting Camden called it the "Biggest Little City in the World" in promotional literature.

# 1916

On January 10, an explosion at the Du Pont gunpowder factory at Carney's Point on the Delaware River killed five workers.

On June 19, the federal government mobilized three infantry regiments, one squadron of cavalry, two batteries of field artillery, one signal corps company, one field hospital and one ambulance company of the New Jersey National Guard for duty on the Mexican border in the wake of the crisis caused by Revolutionary leader Pancho Villa's raid into New Mexico. The units assembled at the National Guard Training Center at Sea Girt on June 21 and traveled from there to Douglas, Arizona, for border duty. They returned to New Jersey at the end of the year.

Between July 1 and July 16, there were a series of deadly shark attacks along the New Jersey shore. On July 1, a swimmer bled to death after being pulled out of the surf at Beach Haven with shredded legs. On July 6, a hotel employee in Spring Lake was attacked and also bled to death. The next attacks occurred farther north in Matawan Creek on July 12, killing a young boy and a rescuer trying to save him. The last victim, attacked a short time later close by, was brought to a hospital and survived. The series of attacks by "the Jersey man-eater" made national news and raised fears up and down the East Coast. The species of shark

Elizabeth "Lizzie" Coleman White, working in conjunction with Frederick Corville at Whitesbog in the Pine Barrens, produced the first cultivated crop of blueberries.

## 1917

On January 11, the Kingsland ammunition plant in Lyndhurst, owned by the Canadian Car and Foundry Company, exploded. Switchboard operator Theresa "Tessie" McNamara was a heroine that day. She stayed at her switchboard calling every building on the site, telling the workers to evacuate, even though exploding shells hit the building she was calling from, and all 1,700 workers escaped. Initially thought to be German sabotage, the explosion was later determined to be the result of an accident.

On the evening of January 12, 400,000 pounds of smokeless powder exploded at the Du Pont plant at Haskell, in Passaic County. Remarkably,

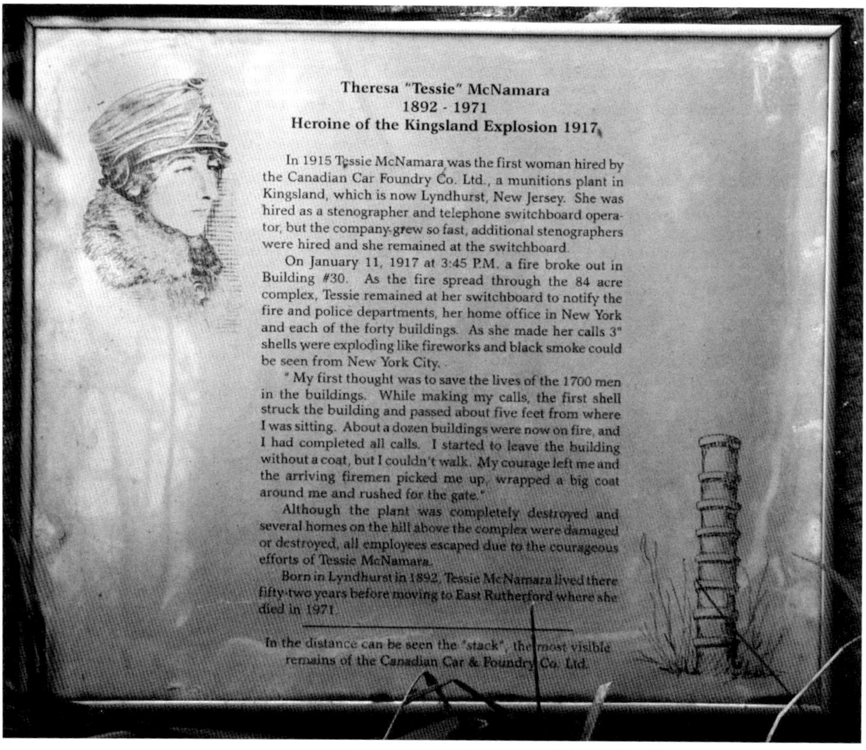


This Kingsland plaque commemorates the disaster's heroine. *James M. Madden.*

only two employees were reported missing and twelve injured. The effects of the blast resonated for a 150-mile radius in New York and New Jersey. Shocks were reportedly felt as far away as Albany.

On April 5, a fire triggered by defective wiring broke out at the Asbury Park beachfront Natatorium, a two-story Greco-Roman-style indoor bathing pavilion. Within minutes, a huge burst of flames engulfed the structure. Pushed by winds that created an "exploding bomb" of destruction, the fire headed toward the heart of the city, engulfing wood-frame hotels, boardinghouses and residences. By the time courageous firefighters subdued the blaze, four city blocks were destroyed.

The United States declared war on Germany on April 6.

New Jersey suffragist Alice Paul and members of her National Women's Party picketed the White House as "silent sentinels" in favor of women's suffrage. With the advent of World War I, and the appearance of "Kaiser Wilson" signs, mobs attacked the women, claiming they were unpatriotic. Paul and her fellow picketers were arrested and sent to a jail in Virginia, where they were abused, and some, including Paul, who went on hunger strikes, were force-fed. Authorities tried to have Paul declared insane but failed as the public and politicians began to call for her release. Once released, having gained public sympathy, she successfully campaigned for the passage of the Nineteenth Amendment granting women the vote.

At the outbreak of World War I, some elements of the New Jersey National Guard were mobilized to guard bridges, railroads and other critical sites.

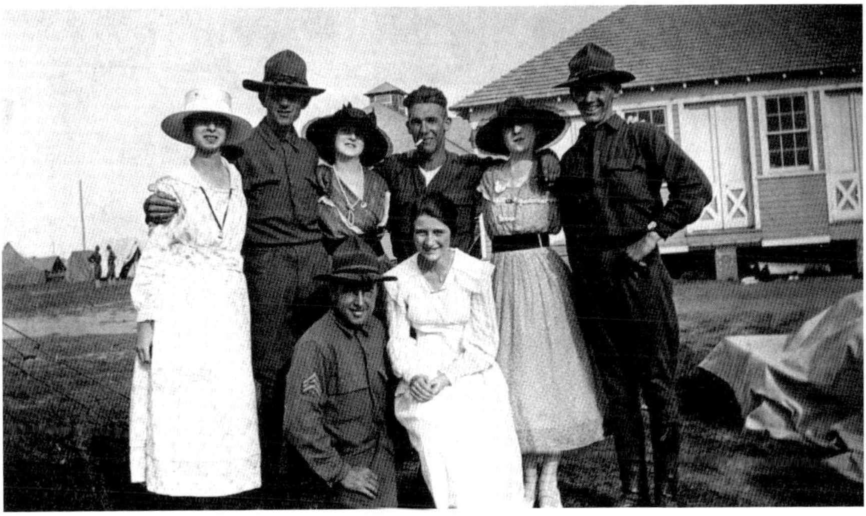

National Guard soldiers, wives and sweethearts at Sea Girt 1917. *NGMMNJ.*

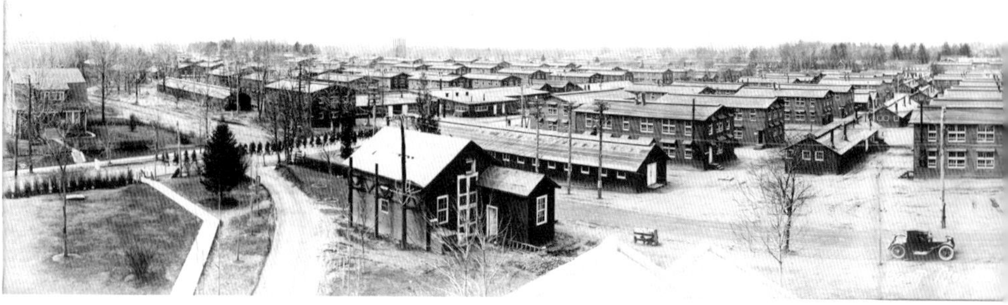

Camp Merritt in Bergen County. *NGMMNJ.*

The Guard's engineer battalion was detailed to lay out Camp Dix, a massive new training center that would have 1,600 buildings within a year. The naval militia reported to Brooklyn and Philadelphia for ship duty.

The remainder of the National Guard was mobilized at Sea Girt on July 25. Most New Jersey National Guard units were subsequently assigned to the Twenty-ninth Division, along with National Guardsmen from Maryland, Virginia and the District of Columbia. The division was organized and trained at Camp McClellan, Alabama.

Two months after the United States' entry into World War I, the first troop transports headed for Europe left Hoboken. Hoboken had a strong German American tradition, and soldiers were ordered to patrol the city in fear that enemy sympathizers might engage in sabotage. Hoboken effectively became a military town as the leading port of embarkation for Europe used by American soldiers for the duration of World War I. Of the approximately 2 million American troops that sailed to Europe, 1.6 million left from the Hudson County city, considered part of the Port of New York. One account states that chaplains conducted as many as forty marriages a day for departing soldiers.

New Jersey's National Guardsmen, ironically, left for France from Newport News, Virginia.

On August 20, construction began on Camp Merritt in Cresskill in Bergen County. Conveniently located for rail or water transport to Hoboken, the chief port of embarkation for Europe in World War I, the camp would process over 1 million soldiers either going overseas or returning home before officially closing in January 1920.

In September, Camp Alfred Vail was founded in Monmouth County on the site of the old Monmouth Race Track.

The United States declared war on Austria-Hungary on December 7.

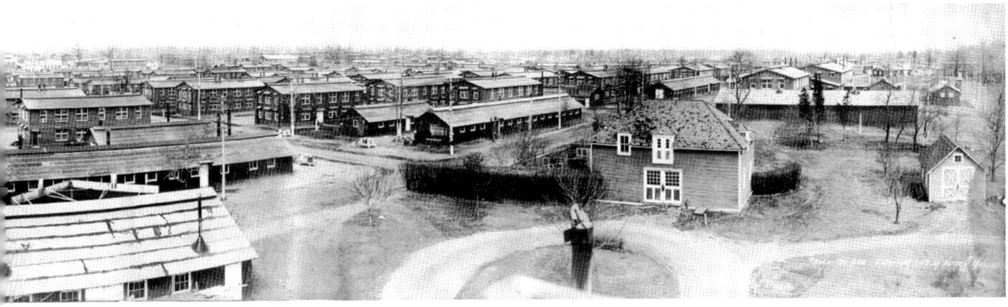

Frank Hague was elected mayor of Jersey City, a position he would hold for the next thirty years. Hague, who delivered a reliable Hudson County Democratic majority that was critical in determining the outcome of New Jersey gubernatorial, U.S. senate and presidential elections, became the most famous political boss of his era.

## 1918

On May 14, Trenton native Needham Roberts and another soldier serving with the segregated African American 369th Infantry Regiment of the New York National Guard ("Harlem Hellfighters"), which had been assigned to the French army because of American army racism, were badly wounded in a German attack but repulsed the enemy using rifles, knives and hand grenades, killing twenty German soldiers in the process. Both men were awarded the *Croix de Guerre* by the French army.

June 2 became known as "Black Sunday" when the German submarine U-151 sank six U.S. ships and damaged two others off the coast of New Jersey in the space of a few hours.

In June and July, the New Jersey National Guardsmen from the Twenty-ninth Division landed in France. The division fought in the Meuse-Argonne offensive in October, advancing over four miles, capturing 2,500 prisoners and losing one-third of its strength.

The New Jersey College for Women opened in New Brunswick on September 18.

On October 4, the T.A. Gillespie Shell Loading Plant, located in the Morgan section of Sayreville, exploded, destroying the munitions manufacturing operation and setting off three days of detonations that destroyed more than three hundred buildings in Sayreville and South Amboy. Sayreville, South

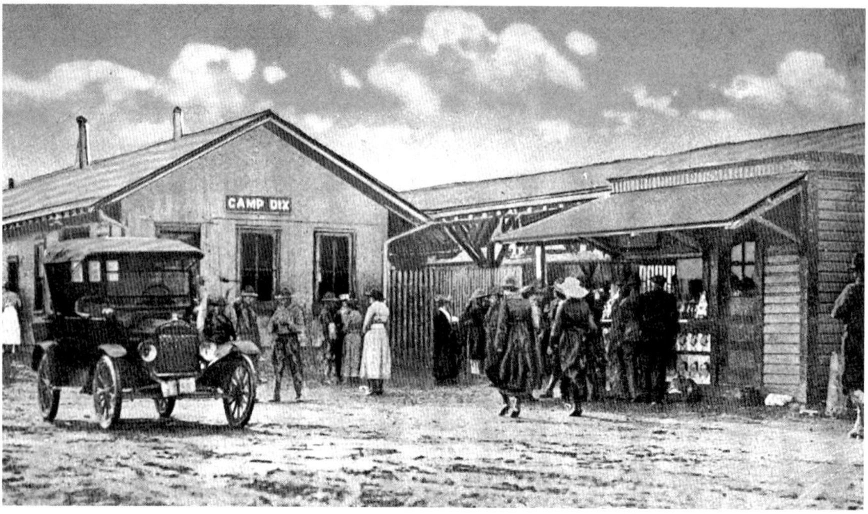


Train station at Camp Dix, 1918. *Joseph G. Bilby.*

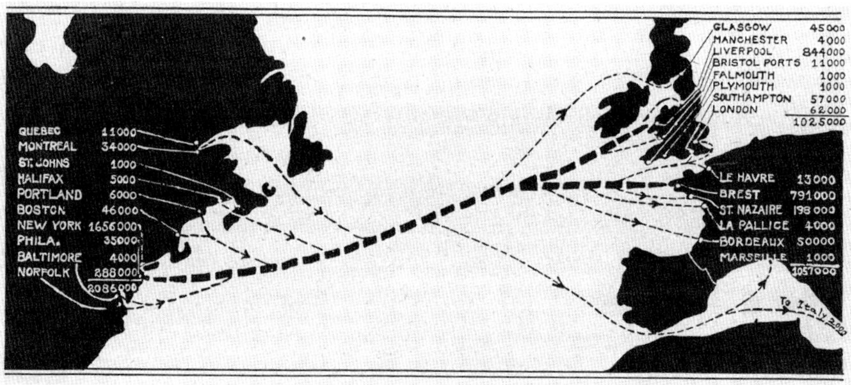


Routes overseas in World War I. Note that most troops departed from Hoboken. *Joseph G. Bilby.*

Amboy and Perth Amboy were evacuated and martial law temporarily established. Over one hundred people are estimated to have perished.

The Seventy-eighth Division, organized from New Jersey and New York draftees at Camp Dix, fought in the St. Mihiel Salient, the Meuse Argonne offensive and Lorraine. Welcomed back to New Jersey in 1919, the Seventy-eighth has remained associated with the state as an Army Reserve unit ever since.

An estimated 130,000 to 150,000 New Jerseyans served in all branches of the armed forces in World War I, and 3,836 died.

## 1919

Ernest Edward "Ernie" Kovacs, radio and early television personality and writer, was born in Trenton.

The Signal Corps School was relocated from Fort Leavenworth to Camp Vail in Monmouth County.

## 1920

The census reported New Jersey's population as 3,155,900.

The Switlik Parachute Company was established by Polish immigrant Stanley Switlik. The company became the largest manufacturer of parachutes in the United States and introduced a number of design innovations, including the substitution of nylon for silk. During World War II, the company manufactured 250,000 parachutes.

Prohibition of the sale of alcohol became the law of the land but was widely ignored in New Jersey, one of three states that had not yet ratified the Eighteenth Amendment. (It did in 1922.) In his successful 1919 campaign, Governor Edward I. Edwards proposed to keep the state "as wet as the Atlantic Ocean." While this did not turn out to be correct, it was not far wrong.

F. Scott Fitzgerald dazzled readers with the novel *This Side of Paradise*, based on his youthful Princeton University days.

## 1921

In April, the Port Authority of New York and New Jersey was founded as a bi-state agency. The new agency's mission was to facilitate transportation and improve transportation facilities in the "Port District" shared by both states, including ports, bridges, tunnels, airports, rail and roads.

The New Jersey state legislature authorized the creation of a state police force of 140 men in legislation passed over Governor Edward I. Edwards's veto. The first superintendent of the force, appointed by Edwards on July 1, was Herbert Norman Schwarzkopf, a Newark-born West Point graduate and former army officer. Schwarzkopf was the father of the successful Gulf War general of the same name.

A heavyweight championship bout between Jack Dempsey and French boxer Georges Carpentier was held on July 2 at Boyle's Thirty Acres in Jersey City. The venue was located near Montgomery Street and Cornelison Avenue, on a plot of marshland owned by John P. Boyle. The well-promoted fight was attended by over eighty thousand spectators and was the first million-dollar gate in boxing history. Dempsey won in the fourth round.

The United States Senate, adamantly opposed to participation in the League of Nations, had refused to approve the Treaty of Versailles, extending America's official involvement in World War I for years after the fighting had actually ceased. The war officially ended for the United States in New Jersey when President Warren Harding, returning from a golf outing at the Somerset Hills Country Club on July 2, signed the Knox-Porter Joint Congressional Resolution declaring hostilities at an end at the home of New Jersey U.S. senator Joseph S. Frelinghuysen in Raritan Borough. The house is long gone, but a small monument marks the spot near the entrance to the Somerville Circle Shopping Center.

Newspaperman Herb Test promoted the first Miss America contest in Atlantic City in September. The winner was sixteen-year-old Margaret Gorman, proclaimed the "most beautiful bathing girl in America."

On November 11, African American Paterson native and recipient of the Medal of Honor for his heroism in the Spanish-American War George H. Wanton was an honorary pallbearer at the interment of the Unknown Soldier at Arlington National Cemetery.

The first broadcast of a World Series game by radio in New Jersey was made from station WJZ in Newark, as an announcer repeated phoned-in reports.

Radio station WDY was opened in Roselle Park by RCA manager David Sarnoff.

The U.S. navy purchased the former Imperial Russian army ammunition testing site in Lakehurst, which had been used by the army as Camp Kendrick after the Bolshevik Revolution, for use as an airship station and renamed it Naval Air Station Lakehurst.

# 1922

On March 17, the Hobart Act, New Jersey's implementation law for the Eighteenth Amendment to the Constitution, was passed. Initial arrests under this law, and the federal Volstead Act, for bootlegging numbered 91 in 1922 but, by 1932, had escalated to 996. There were a total of 4,768 arrests for manufacturing, sale, possession and transportation of alcohol in New Jersey during Prohibition, about 400 of them for traditional "Jersey Lightning" or applejack, most of the latter in Sussex, Warren and Hunterdon Counties.

On September 22, Reverend Edward Wheeler Hall, an Episcopal priest in New Brunswick, was found shot dead along with his mistress, Eleanor Reinhardt Mills, a member of the church choir, in De Russey's Lane in Franklin Township. Suspicion fell on Reverend Hall's wife, Francis, and her brothers, but there were no indictments. The crime became popularly known as the "Hall-Mills Murders."

WOR radio began broadcasting from Newark in February with two hundred watts of power. The station was the first in the eastern United States to schedule fifteen-minute news broadcasts.

# 1923

The first American navy airship, the USS *Shenandoah*, built at Lakehurst Naval Air Station, took to the sky for the first time in September.

Feminist activist Alice Paul successfully agitated for the introduction of an Equal Rights Amendment in Congress. It was introduced in every Congress for the next forty-nine years but never became law.

A state forest fire warden with headquarters in Trenton was appointed, and the state was divided into 372 fire districts.

Upsala College, originally founded in Brooklyn by the Evangelical Lutheran Church in America, acquired a campus in East Orange after a number of moves around the metropolitan area. Declining enrollment and competition with other colleges caused Upsala to close on May 31, 1995.

On July 23, the Felician Sisters founded Immaculate Conception Normal School in Lodi as a two-year college intended to train nuns for careers as teachers. The school began enrolling laywomen in 1964 and became a four-year degree-granting institution in 1967 under the name Felician College. It has been coeducational since 1986.

Glassboro Normal School opened its doors on September 4. It became the Teacher's College at Glassboro in 1937, Glassboro State College in 1958 and then Rowan College in honor of Henry Rowan, who donated $100 million to the school. It was designated as Rowan University in 1997. Rowan College became internationally famous in June 1967, when it served as the site of a summit meeting between President Lyndon B. Johnson and Premier Alexi Kosygin of the Soviet Union.

## 1924

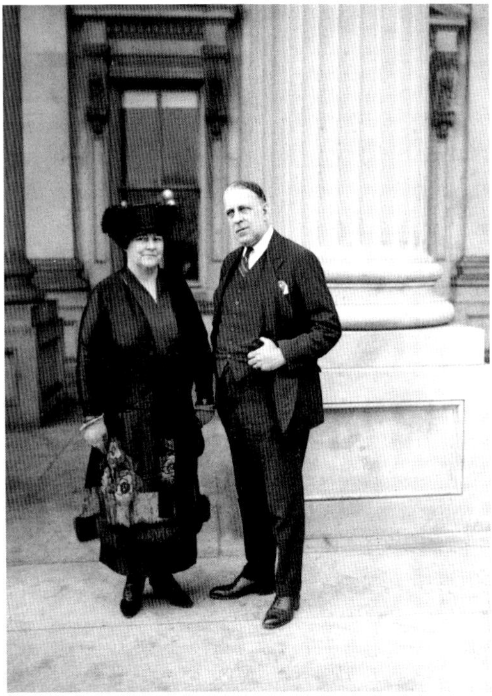

Congresswoman-elect Mary Norton and Senator David I. Walsh of Massachusetts in 1924. *Joseph G. Bilby.*

Long Branch was the site of the Ku Klux Klan's "Tri-State Konklave," hosting Klansmen and Klanswomen from New York, New Jersey and Pennsylvania over the Fourth of July weekend. The Konklave featured Klan parades and sporting events, including a "minister's race" and a march through the streets of the town. The Klan was strong in New Jersey in the 1920s, as rural Protestant New Jerseyans joined not only to ensure continued white supremacy but also to protect "their America" from immigrants, Catholics and Jews. Plagued by scandals and deserted by a populace battered by the Depression, the Klan disintegrated in the 1930s.

The Morris Canal, no longer in active use and described by one New Jersey assemblyman that year as "an open sewer," was finally abandoned. The state took over the canal property, dismantled and sold it. Some sections have been preserved as park space and for historical interest. Part of the canal bed was used for the Newark City Subway, now a light rail route.

Jersey City's Mary Teresa Norton became the first New Jersey woman and the first female Democrat elected to the House of Representatives. She served in the House until 1950.

Maplewood dentist William Lowell, who had hand-carved the prototype three years before, patented the modern golf tee. Although Lowell made a considerable amount of money on his invention, he also spent a lot of it fighting patent infringements over the years since his patent application was not as specific as it could have been.

## 1925

At a gala Asbury Park event attended by some five hundred influential colleagues from around New Jersey, businessman Arthur C. Steinbach presented his architectural masterpiece, the spectacular eight-story Berkeley Carteret, designed by noted New York architect Warren Whitney, a luxury hotel that epitomized elegant vacationing in Asbury Park.

In August, Camp Vail was granted permanent status and renamed Fort Monmouth.

The first traffic circle, the Airport Circle, was built in Pennsauken.

The American Telephone and Telegraph Company established Bell Laboratories, which located some of its most important research facilities in New Jersey, at Holmdel and Whippany. The Whippany location was the site of the first experimental television broadcast in the United States in 1927.

## 1926

On May 31, famed sculptor Gutzon Borglum's massive bronze *Wars of America* statue, representing every conflict the United States participated in from the Revolution to World War I and comprising figures of forty-two humans and two horses, was unveiled in Newark's Military Park. The statue was added to the National Register of Historic Places in 1994.

Irwin Allen Ginsburg, famed "Beat Generation" poet who would win a landmark acquittal in an obscenity case brought by the federal government, was born in Paterson on June 3.

On July 10, the most damaging lightning strike in U.S. history hit the Naval Ammunition Depot at Lake Denmark in Morris County; nineteen people were killed, thirty-eight were injured and an estimated $75 million in damage was reported following the subsequent explosion.

Continued newspaper speculation on the Hall-Mills murders led Governor A. Harry Moore to request a new inquiry into the case. The investigation led to indictments of Frances Hall and her brothers for murder and a trial that began on November 3 and lasted thirty days. Although the accused had the motive and ability to commit the murders, the evidence to convict them, especially the erratic testimony of the "pig woman," Jane Gibson, whose claim to be a witness provided a prime rationale for the indictments, was not convincing to the jury, and they were acquitted.

On December 21, a force of state troopers, summoned to a farmhouse in Jutland, New Jersey, on a cattle dealer's false complaint that the farmers, eccentric brothers Timothy and James Meaney and their sister Beatrice, were abusing their livestock, fired hundreds of rounds at the house, killing Beatrice and seriously wounding James in what became known in local lore as the "Battle of Jutland," evoking the World War I naval battle of the same name. Area farmers, backed by political figures and newspapers as prominent as the *New York Times*, were outraged and called on Governor A. Harry Moore to order an investigation of the incident. The investigation resulted in the indictment, trial and conviction of two of the troopers.

The Delaware Bridge, a 1,750-foot span linking Camden and Philadelphia, was dedicated by President Calvin Coolidge. The bridge, built at a cost of $36 million, included six car lanes and two electric railroad lanes. It was rededicated as the Benjamin Franklin Bridge in 1956.

Bell Laboratories created a system of making motion pictures with integral sound.

New Jersey reached a total of 500,000 telephones in service.

# 1927

On June 1, three earthquake shocks were felt along the New Jersey coast from Sandy Hook to Toms River. The highest intensities were observed

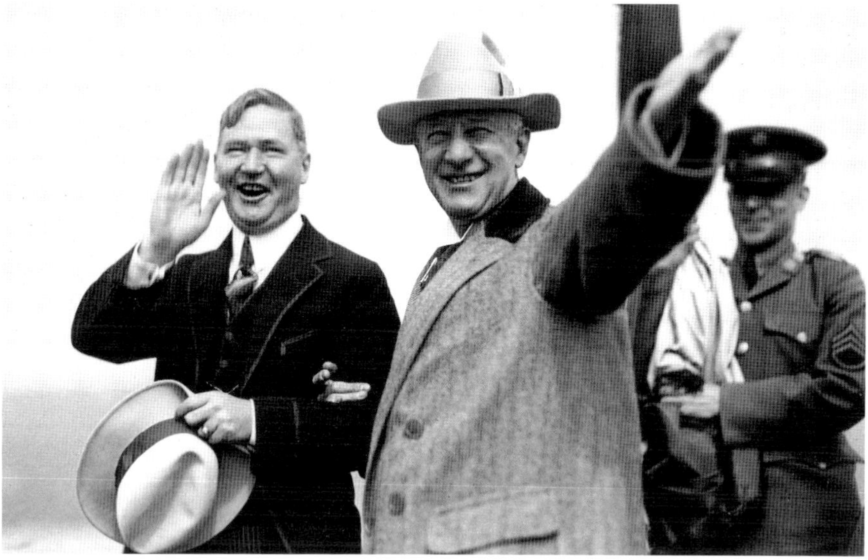

Governors A. Harry Moore of New Jersey and Al Smith of New York at the groundbreaking ceremony for the George Washington Bridge. *Joseph G. Bilby.*

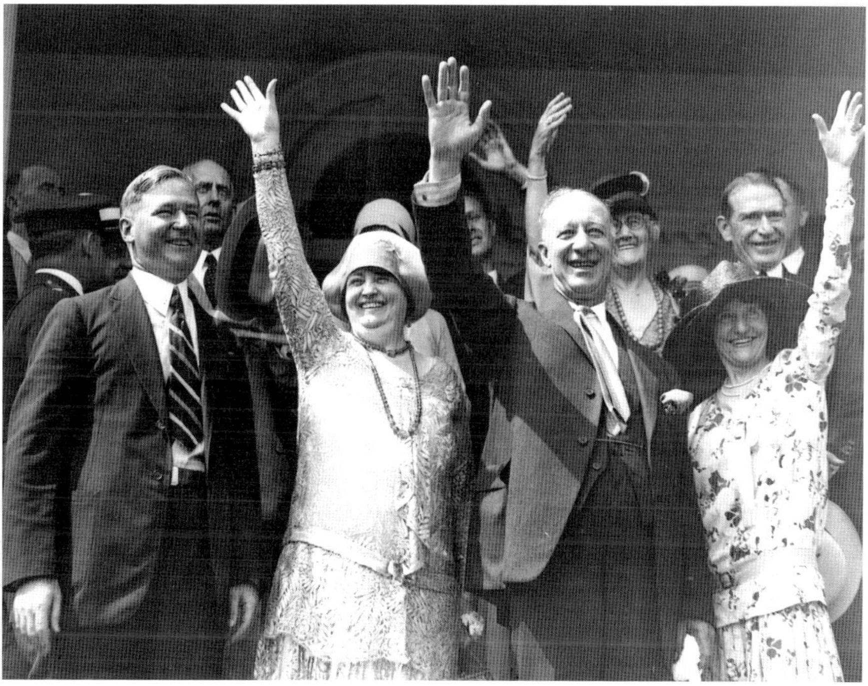

Al Smith, A. Harry Moore and their wives at Sea Girt, 1928. *Joseph G. Bilby.*

from Asbury Park to Long Branch, where chimneys fell, plaster cracked and objects were thrown from shelves.

Asbury Park bolstered its reputation as a regional entertainment center with the opening of the Mayfair, a million-dollar Spanish Moorish–style movie palace.

On September 21, New Jersey governor A. Harry Moore and New York governor Al Smith met for the groundbreaking ceremony for the Fort Lee Bridge, later to be named the George Washington Bridge.

The Holland Tunnel between New York and Jersey City was opened on November 13.

## 1928

On July 12, Captain Emilio Carranza, "Mexico's Lindbergh," crashed his plane in the New Jersey Pine Barrens while returning to Mexico from a goodwill flight to New York. Carranza was killed in the crash. His body was recovered by members of a local American Legion Post the following day and brought to Buzby's store in Chatsworth. Mexican schoolchildren contributed money to build a monument at the crash site in Tabernacle, and there is a memorial service held there each year, conducted by the Mexican consuls to New York and Philadelphia and the American Legion.

On July 22, humorist Will Rogers landed in a plane on the drill field at Sea Girt National Guard Camp, where the governors of New Jersey spent their summer months. Rogers had dinner with Governor Moore and the governor's wife before going on to a speaking engagement in Ocean Grove.

On August 2, following a Democratic Party rally, famed female aviator Amelia Earhart performed aerial acrobatics above the National Guard Camp at Sea Girt, where Governor Moore was spending the summer, and then landed on the drill field.

On August 25, Jersey City mayor Frank Hague and Governor Moore held a massive political rally on behalf of Democratic presidential candidate and New York governor Al Smith at the Sea Girt National Guard Camp. The crowd was estimated at eighty thousand people.

On August 25, Richard E. Byrd's expedition to Antarctica set out from Hoboken.

In October, the Jersey Central Railroad initiated its Blue Comet luxury train service between Jersey City and Atlantic City.

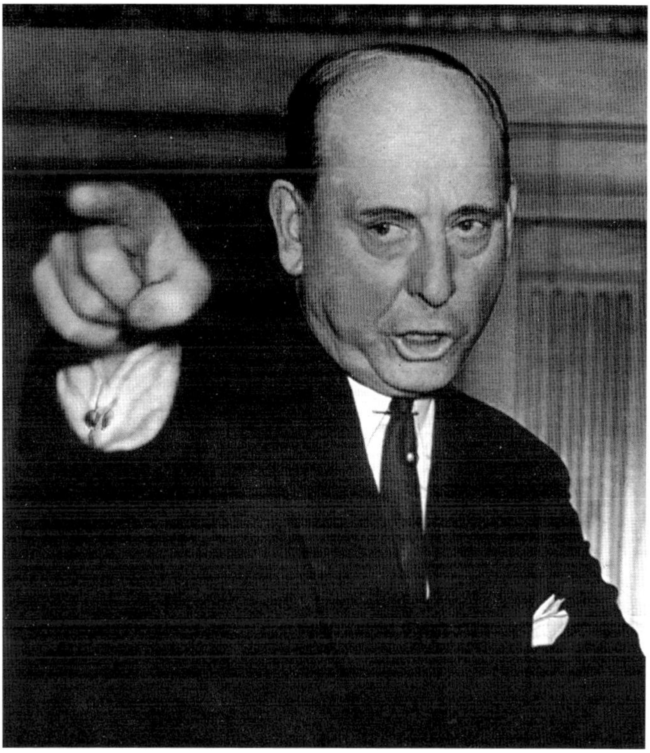

Frank Hague, mayor of Jersey City and New Jersey and America's best-known political boss in the 1930s. *James M. Madden.*

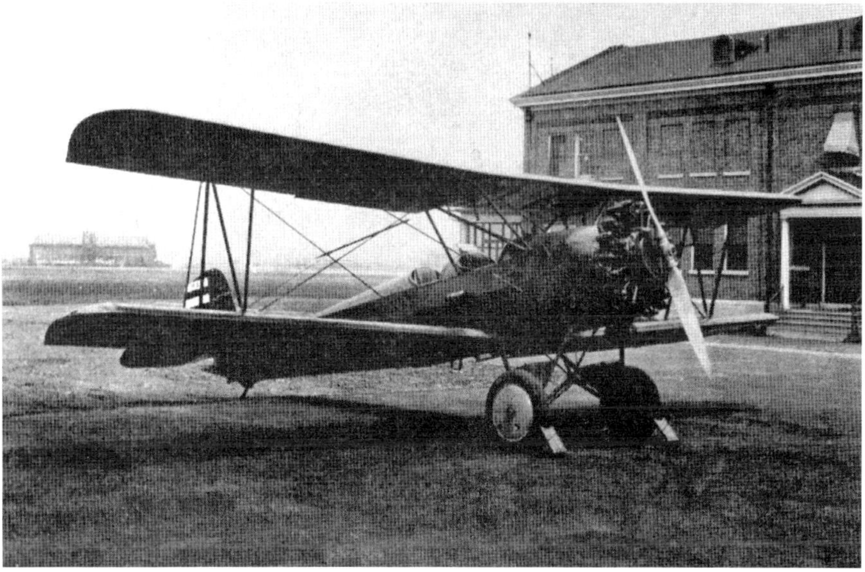

Newark Airport in 1931, with a National Guard observation plane. *NGMMNJ.*

Entrepreneur Frank P. Gravatt, an Atlantic City hotel builder, was intrigued by the daring performance of a popular horse diving feat and lured the act to Atlantic City, where the Diving Horse became one of the biggest crowd-pleasers at the city's Steel Pier. During the performance, horses galloped up a runway forty-five feet high and dove into a pool of water, a female rider perched on each horse's back.

Construction began on Newark Airport, located in the meadowlands between Newark and Elizabeth.

The Goethals Bridge spanning the Arthur Kill between Elizabeth and Staten Island opened. The bridge was named for Major General George Goethals, the engineer who built the Panama Canal and was the Port Authority of New York and New Jersey's first consulting engineer.

The 119th Observation Squadron, the first New Jersey National Guard unit to be assigned aircraft, was created, with unit headquarters established at Newark Airport, then under construction.

After previously donating 10,500 acres to the State of New Jersey to found High Point State Park, the Kuser family donated High Point Monument, a 221-foot-tall obelisk honoring New Jersey's war veterans, to the state. High Point, the summit of Kittatinny Ridge in Sussex County, is the highest elevation in New Jersey.

# 1929

On January 29, the first seeing-eye guide dog school in America, Dorothy Harrison Eustis' Morris Township Seeing Eye Incorporated, received a charter.

Trenton celebrated its 250th anniversary with a massive parade and optimistic speeches predicting a bright future for the prosperous city. The festive event was held on October 29—the day of the stock market crash that plunged the nation into the Great Depression.

The first cloverleaf highway intersection, based on a design borrowed from Argentina, was built in Woodbridge.

Newark Airport opened with two runways built on seventy acres reclaimed from a salt marsh.

# 1930

The census reported New Jersey's population as 4,041,334. The number of foreign-born New Jerseyans dropped to 21 percent of the population, down from 25 percent in the census of 1910.

Astronaut Edwin E. "Buzz" Aldrin was born in Montclair on January 20.

On September 20, Prohibition agent John J. Finiello was murdered during a raid on the Rising Sun Brewery in Elizabeth.

The New Jersey state police developed a teletype system to provide instant communication between law enforcement agencies in New Jersey and those in other states.

Eighteen tanks and dockage facilities at the Gulf Oil Refining Company in Bayonne were destroyed by fire and explosions, resulting in a $3 million property loss and an ecological disaster, the latter largely overlooked during the era. At the height of the disaster, blazing barges pursued by fireboats and tugs drifted into New York Harbor.

In response to African American New Jerseyans who wished to organize a New Jersey National Guard unit in a segregated military, which was denied

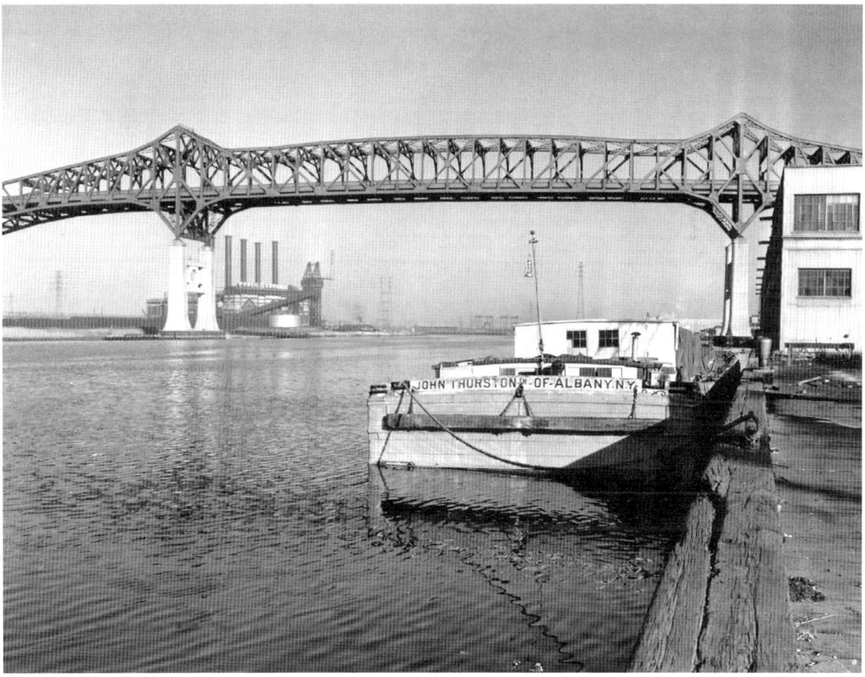


The Pulaski Skyway Bridge over the Hackensack River in 1939. *Joseph G. Bilby.*

them by the federal government, the state legislature passed Chapter 149, Laws of 1930, authorizing the "organization and equipment of a battalion of Negro infantry" at state expense.

Today's New Jersey City University opened as the New Jersey State Normal School, a two-year teacher training institution. It evolved into a four-year institution in 1935 and became Jersey City State College in 1958. In 1998, the school was granted university status.

Construction began on an elevated roadway, or viaduct, between Newark and Jersey City, with integral bridges crossing the Passaic and Hackensack Rivers. Completed in 1932 and originally called the "Diagonal Highway," it was renamed the Pulaski Skyway in honor of Casimir Pulaski, Polish volunteer officer in the American Revolution.

## 1931

On October 18, Thomas Alva Edison died in West Orange.

The Port of New York Authority announced that the soon-to-be-opened Hudson River Bridge connecting New York and New Jersey would be named the George Washington Bridge.

On October 25, the George Washington Bridge was opened for traffic.

On November 26, the magazine *Engineering News-Record* noted that New Jersey, a state with a "major intersection problem," was on the way to solving it with the introduction of the "cloverleaf," which it cited as an "outstanding example of New Jersey Intersection practice."

Marlboro State Psychiatric Hospital was opened in Monmouth County to relieve overcrowding in the state's other psychiatric facilities.

Unaware they were fighting a battle they would soon lose, New Jersey members of the Anti-Saloon League met in Newark to form the Citizens' Federation for Temperance and Law Observance.

## 1932

On January 19, Governor A. Harry Moore chose to be sworn into office at the new and magnificent Art Deco–style Trenton War Memorial building, a source of pride in Trenton as the country struggled with the deepening Depression.

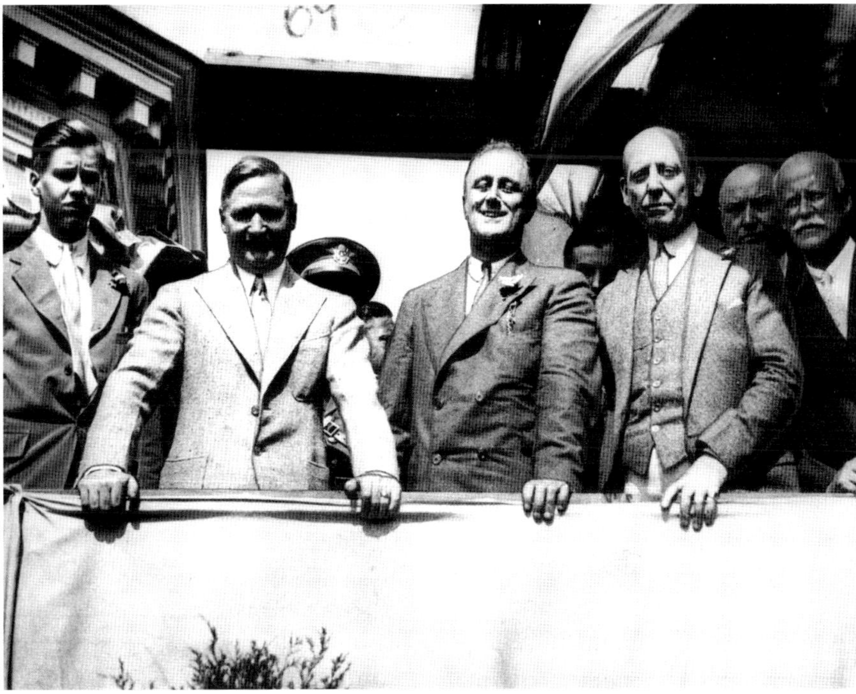

Franklin D. Roosevelt at Sea Girt with Governor A. Harry Moore and Jersey City mayor Frank Hague in 1932. *Franklin D. Roosevelt Library.*

Twenty-month-old Charles A. Lindbergh Jr. was kidnapped from his home in Hopewell, New Jersey, on March 1 between 8:00 and 10:00 p.m.

On March 13, the *Trenton Sunday Times-Advertiser* announced that Newark Airport was the busiest airport in the world, handling more than a quarter of the country's air traffic.

On August 28, in his first stop after winning the Democratic Party presidential nomination, Franklin Delano Roosevelt addressed a huge rally of supporters in Sea Girt at the National Guard Camp. The crowd, estimated at over 100,000 people, had been assembled by Jersey City mayor and Hudson County political boss Frank Hague.

James "Jimmy Buff" Racioppi introduced the "Italian hot dog," which he credited his grandmother with inventing, in his store on Fourteenth Avenue and South Ninth Street in Newark. The sandwich, unique to Newark, was composed of a deep-fried hot dog (or two for a "double") topped with fried peppers, onions and potatoes, encased in a quarter (or half for a "double") of a circular "pizza bread" loaf. The original store is gone, but there are

The American Newspaper Guild conducted a successful strike against the *Newark Ledger*, in the nation's first large-scale strike of newspapermen. The victory not only established the guild as a labor power but also broke ground for the subsequent CIO drive to organize white-collar workers.

The New Jersey Agricultural Experiment station developed the famed "Rutgers Tomato" hybrid.

## 1935

On February 13, after eleven hours of deliberation, a jury found Bruno Richard Hauptmann guilty of the kidnapping and murder of the Lindbergh baby.

On May 6, President Franklin D. Roosevelt established the Works Progress Administration (WPA), a coordinated federal, state and local enterprise intended to both provide jobs for those unemployed by the Depression and perform vital community services, from infrastructure construction to cultural affairs. Large numbers of New Jerseyans gained employment through the WPA, and much of its work still stands. New Jersey ranked among the top ten states in numbers of WPA jobs.

On June 2, Amelia Earhart made the first public parachute jump at the Switlik Parachute Company's jump-training tower at the Switlik farm in Ocean County. The tower was designed by her husband, George Palmer Putnam.

On October 16, Governor Harold G. Hoffman visited Bruno Richard Hauptmann in his cell and interviewed him.

On October 23, mobster Arthur Flegenheimer, better known as "Dutch Schultz," was murdered along with three of his associates at the Palace Chop House in Newark.

Advertising executive George H. Gallup founded the American Institute of Public Opinion in Princeton. The following year, the Gallup Poll accurately predicted the presidential election victory of Franklin D. Roosevelt.

Burlington County detective Ellis Parker was encouraged by Governor Hoffman to investigate the Lindbergh baby kidnapping and, shortly afterward, produced a confession signed by disbarred Trenton attorney Paul H. Wendel. Wendel subsequently recanted, claiming he was held and beaten by men hired by Parker until he signed a confession. Parker was tried and convicted and died in prison in 1940.

# 1936

In January, Governor Hoffman stayed the execution of Bruno Richard Hauptmann, ordering Colonel Schwartzkopf of the state police to investigate the case further.

In the depths of the Depression, the Budget Advisory Committee advised Governor Hoffman that "as to our local governments the general financial situation is little short of tragic."

On April 21, a group of unemployed people, calling themselves the "Army of Unoccupation," took over the statehouse in Trenton in a protest demonstration, demanding that the state relief fund, which had run out of money, be funded. Legislators gathered up their papers and quickly left the building, and by the following day, the group had grown from 20 to 250 people. The demonstrators left the statehouse peacefully on April 29 but promised that they would be heard from in the next election.

On April 23, Bruno Richard Hauptman was executed at the New Jersey state prison in Trenton for the Lindbergh baby's kidnapping and murder.

A temperature of 110 degrees Fahrenheit was reported at Runyon, in Middlesex County, on July 10. It was the hottest temperature ever recorded in New Jersey history to that date.

Two farms owned by the Campbell Soup Company of Camden, one at Riverton and the other in Georgia, sold fifty million tomato plants to New Jersey farmers.

Governor Hoffman fired state police superintendent Schwartzkopf due to disagreements over the Lindbergh case.

New Jersey passed a law directed at the German-American Bund, a pro-Nazi organization that was particularly strong in the state. The law prohibited "hatred, abuse, violence or hostility" against any group because of race or religion.

# 1937

The German airship *Hindenburg* exploded and burst into flames over Lakehurst on May 6. Thirty-six of the ninety-seven passengers and crew on board died in the thirty-four-second-long disaster. The cause was never accurately determined, although sabotage and static electricity have been offered as possibilities.

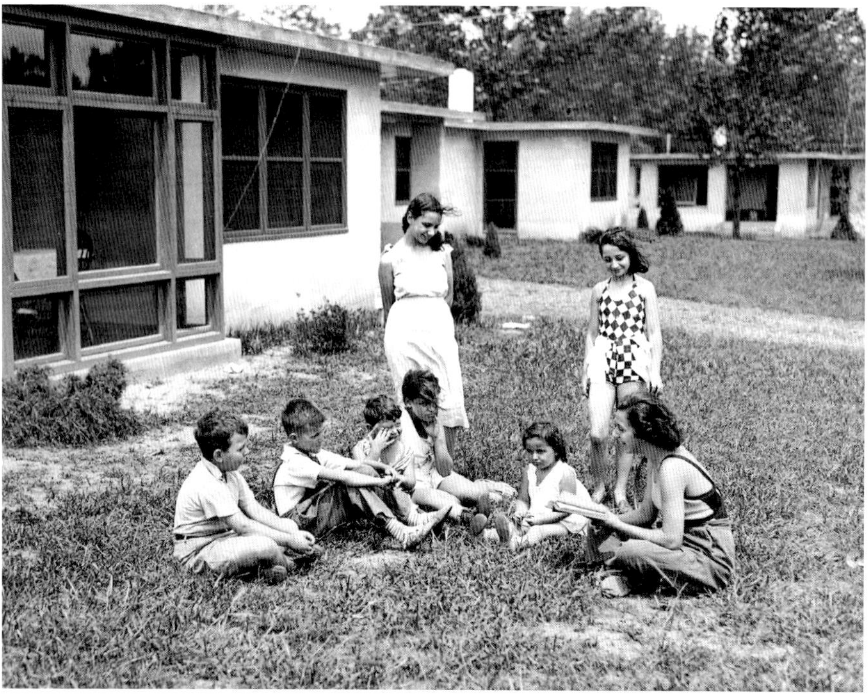

Jersey Homesteads in 1937. *Joseph G. Bilby.*

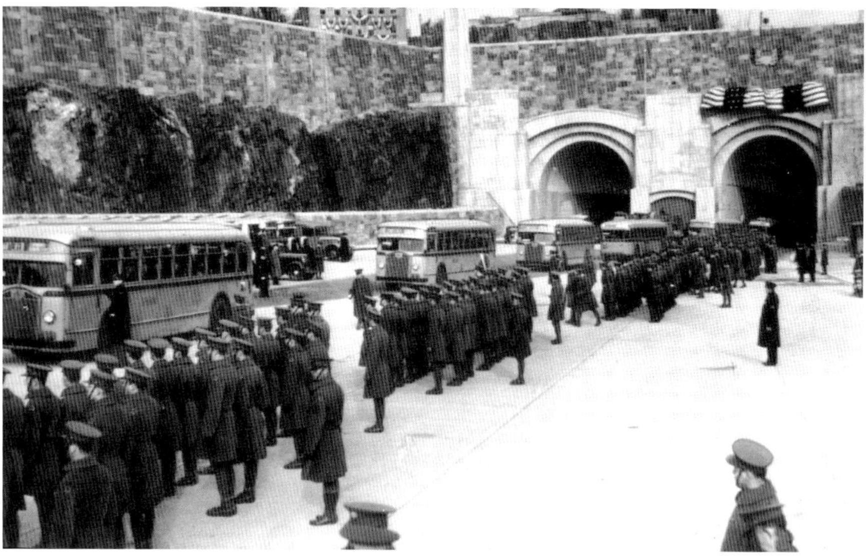

Opening ceremonies for the Lincoln Tunnel in 1937. *Joseph G. Bilby.*

On May 29, the borough of Jersey Homesteads was officially created in Millstone Township in Monmouth County, although construction had begun in 1936. The community, supported by Albert Einstein and artist Ben Shahn, was planned as a refuge for unemployed urban Jewish garment workers from New York City in a place where they would own a cooperative farm and factory. The cooperatives failed, but the town did not and was renamed Roosevelt in honor of the late president Franklin D. Roosevelt on November 9, 1945.

Camp Nordland, a summer camp and resort for German-American Bund members, was opened in the foothills of rural Andover Township on July 18. Bund members dressed in Nazi-style uniforms and gave the fascist extended-arm salute, and the camp became the site of fanatical rallies filled with venomous rhetoric promoting a "Gentile ruled" America.

The Lincoln Tunnel between New York and New Jersey was completed and dedicated on December 21 and opened to traffic the following day.

## 1938

A 131-foot Art Deco tower erected in honor of Thomas Edison in Menlo Park (in today's Edison Township) was dedicated on February 11. It was placed on the National Register of Historic Places in 1979.

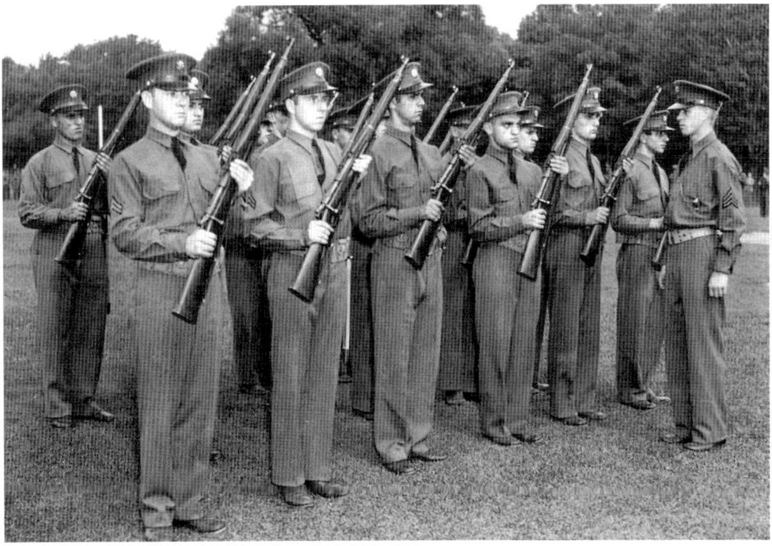

Soldiers of the 113th Infantry in Newark training after 1940 mobilization. *NGMMNJ.*

On October 30, the Orson Welles radio broadcast of "War of the Worlds," on the *Mercury Theater of the Air*, led some people to believe that Martians had landed in West Windsor. Princeton psychologist Hadley Cantril published a study of the incident's "psychology of panic" in 1947. Some recent scholars dispute the extent of the panic.

On December 12, Concetta Maria Franconero was born in Newark. Known professionally as Connie Francis, she was one of the most popular singers in America between 1958 and 1964, when she recorded thirty-five songs that made the Top Forty and also starred in a number of films.

## 1939

In March, Camp Dix was officially renamed Fort Dix.

On July 18, radio engineer Edwin H. Armstrong began the first FM (frequency modulation) radio station, W2XMN, at Alpine, in Bergen County.

DuMont Laboratories was licensed to begin experimental telecasts, although commercial television broadcasting was still nine years away. The station eventually became WABD, Channel 5.

The return of parimutuel betting on horse races, banned in New Jersey since the 1890s, was approved by the voters in a constitutional amendment referendum.

Caldwell College for Women was founded by the Catholic Sisters of Saint Dominic. The college was fully accredited in 1954 and became coeducational in 1985.

## 1940

The census reported New Jersey's population as 4,160,165.

In August, the federal government called the New Jersey National Guard's Forty-fourth Division, along with most other National Guard units across the country, to active duty. The Forty-fourth was activated on September 16 and was assigned to Fort Dix.

On September 12, a massive explosion of 297,000 pounds of gunpowder at the Hercules Powder Plant in Kenville killed fifty-one workers. Another two hundred were injured. Speculation was rife that the cause of the explosion was sabotage, as World War II was raging in Europe, but the cause was never proven.

## 1941

The 102nd Cavalry of the New Jersey National Guard was called to active duty on January 6 and was sent to Fort Jackson, South Carolina, for training. The 102nd went on to be the first New Jersey National Guard unit to go overseas.

A Jersey cow named You'll Do Lobelia, which became a media sensation by appearing as Borden's cartoon character Elsie the Cow at the World's Fair, was fatally injured and had to be euthanized on April 16 when her custom eighteen-wheeler "Cowdillac" was hit from behind by another truck in Rahway.

New Jersey attorney general David Willentz authorized a County Sheriff's Office raid on Camp Nordland, the German American Bund resort in Sussex County. On April 30, County Sheriff Denton Quick, assisted by ten deputized American Legion members, raided the camp and closed it for good. Turned over to Andover Township, it was later used as a park area and for municipal purposes, including, ironically, the township police department headquarters.

On December 7, the Imperial Japanese Navy attacked the U.S. naval base at Pearl Harbor, Hawaii. On December 8, the United States declared war on Japan. On December 11, 1941, the United States declared war on Germany and Italy in response to those nations' declarations of war on the United States following the Japanese attack on Pearl Harbor.

Governor Charles Edison, son of the inventor, was the last New Jersey governor to summer at Sea Girt in the "Little White House."

## 1942

On January 15, the British oil tanker *Coimbra* was sunk by a German submarine one hundred miles off Sandy Hook, signaling the arrival of World War II in New Jersey waters.

Beatrice Alice Hicks, who was born in Orange in 1919, became the first female engineer hired by Western Electric.

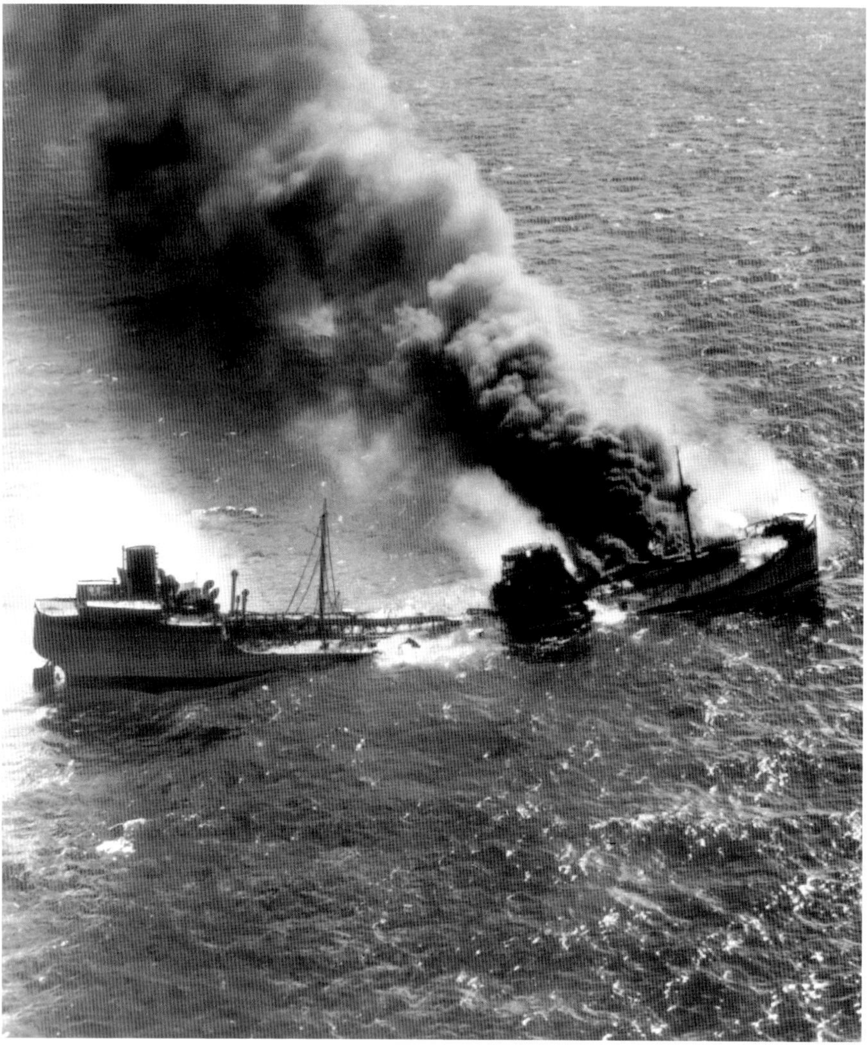

The SS *R.P. Resor* on fire after being torpedoed off the New Jersey coast. *Joseph G. Bilby.*

On February 28, a German submarine torpedoed the SS *R.P. Resor* eighteen miles east of Lavallette on a bright moonlit night. The explosion and "spectacular, towering fire" was so great that it could be seen from shore, and the Shark River Lifeboat Station was the first to report the incident. Only two men survived. The following morning, the World War I–era destroyer USS *Jacob Jones* was torpedoed while searching for more survivors. There were only twelve survivors of the sinking of the *Jones*.

Camp Kilmer, named for New Jersey poet Joyce Kilmer, who was killed in World War I, was established on 1,500 acres of land near New Brunswick for the purpose of staging troops on their way overseas. It also served as a POW camp holding more than one thousand German and Italian prisoners later in the war.

On October 24, U.S. Marine Corps sergeant John Basilone of Raritan, commanding a machine gun section defending Henderson Field on Guadalcanal, held off an attack by three thousand Japanese soldiers, fighting for three days and nights without sleep and ending the battle firing at them with his .45-caliber automatic pistol. For his heroism, Basilone was awarded the Medal of Honor.

The National Guard's Sea Girt camp was leased to the federal government, which used it for Signal Corps training as a substation of Fort Monmouth through 1945.

As with many coastal resort cities, most notably Atlantic City, Asbury Park's major hotels became barracks during World War II. The U.S. Army Signal Corps took over the Kingsley Arms, while the navy leased the Monterey and Berkeley-Carteret and turned them into "in transit" quarters for British and Commonwealth sailors between "Lend-Lease" ship assignments.

The 113th Infantry Regiment, New Jersey National Guard, was relieved from its assignment to the National Guard's 44th Division and reassigned to coastal defense. The regiment was spread out in company-sized detachments from Long Island to Delaware. Later in the war, the 113th was assigned to various posts in the United States as a training unit.

Dr. Peter Sammartino and his wife, Sylvia, founded a junior college in Rutherford that would eventually become Fairleigh Dickinson University.

# 1943

On February 3, 1943, the troop ship USAT *Dorchester*, with 904 men aboard, was torpedoed on its way to Greenland. Four chaplains on board—one Jewish, two Protestant and one Catholic—gave up their lifejackets to soldiers, joined arms, said prayers and went down with the ship. There were 230 survivors. The Catholic chaplain, Father John Washington, was a New Jerseyan, born in Newark in 1908. Washington was a graduate of Seton Hall University and Darlington Seminary. At the time he joined the army, he was assigned to St. Stephen's parish in Kearny. Washington and the other three chaplains were posthumously awarded the Distinguished Service Cross and the Purple Heart. There is a monument to Father Washington at Saint Rose of Lima Church, his home parish, on Orange Street in Newark and another to all four chaplains in Kearny.

The battleship USS *New Jersey*, built at the Philadelphia Naval Shipyard, was launched on December 7, commissioned and subsequently served in the Pacific during World War II and in Korea, Vietnam and the Middle East. The *New Jersey*, now a floating museum in Camden, became the most decorated American battleship in history.

Civil defense director Leonard Dreyfuss reported to Governor Charles Edison that there were "262,000 citizens engaged in the protective services of the state, all volunteers." Their jobs included "air raid warning systems, auxiliary police, auxiliary firemen, fire watchers, medical services, etc."

MGM movie star Judy Garland entertained enthusiastic GIs stationed at Sandy Hook's Fort Hancock.

Rutgers graduate student Albert I. Schatz and his professor, Selman Waksman, discovered the antibiotic streptomycin, the first effective treatment for tuberculosis. They were awarded the Nobel Prize in Physiology and Medicine in 1952.

A squadron of the 102$^{nd}$ Cavalry was transferred from England to North Africa, where it was eventually redesignated the 117$^{th}$ Cavalry. The unit participated in the North African and Italian campaigns and then in the invasion of southern France.

# 1944

On September 14, the "Great Atlantic Hurricane of '44" (unlike today, hurricanes then went unnamed) struck New Jersey with winds of ninety-six miles per hour and generated a storm surge that lifted vacation cottages off their foundations and deposited them blocks away and wrecked boardwalks all along the coast.

The 102$^{nd}$ Cavalry participated in the Normandy invasion, landing on June 8. In the following weeks, Sergeant Curtis Culin of Cranford and the 102$^{nd}$ devised the "Rhino Plow," a device that, attached to the front of tanks, cut through hedgerows in Normandy, vitally assisting the allied armies in breaking out of their beachhead. The 102$^{nd}$ fought its way across Europe, on the way gaining the honor of being the first United States unit to enter Paris in August 1944.

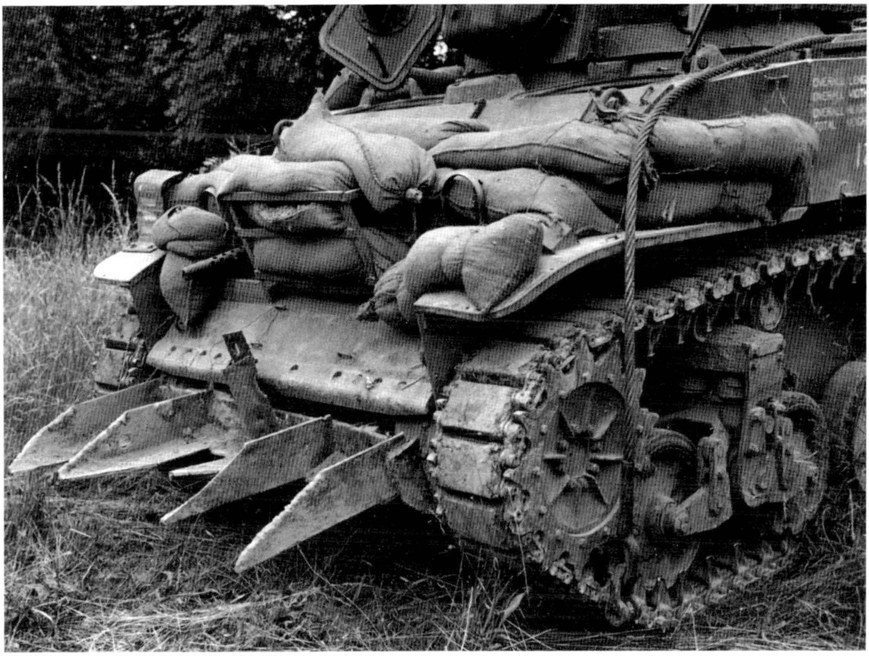

Curtis Culin's "Rhino Plow." *U.S. Army Military History Center.*

After serving in various posts around the country, being reduced and then increased in strength, the Forty-fourth Division was shipped overseas at the end of August and landed in Cherbourg, France, in early September. The division fought in the Rhineland and Alsace and was in combat for 190 days, earning three Distinguished Unit Citations. The Forty-fourth was demobilized at the end of the war.

## 1945

Although stationed stateside following the award of his Medal of Honor, Sergeant John Basilone requested permission to return to the battlefront. On February 28, on the island of Iwo Jima, Basilone personally destroyed a Japanese strong point, using hand grenades and other explosives. Shortly afterward, while guiding a tank out of harm's way, he was killed in action. For his heroism, Sergeant Basilone was posthumously awarded the Navy Cross, the Marine Corps' second highest decoration.

The New Jersey legislature enacted the nation's first statewide civil rights enforcement statute, which prohibited discrimination in employment, housing and places of public accommodation on the basis of race, national origin, sex, age, disability, creed and other "protected categories."

Rutgers was officially named as New Jersey's state university.

## 1946

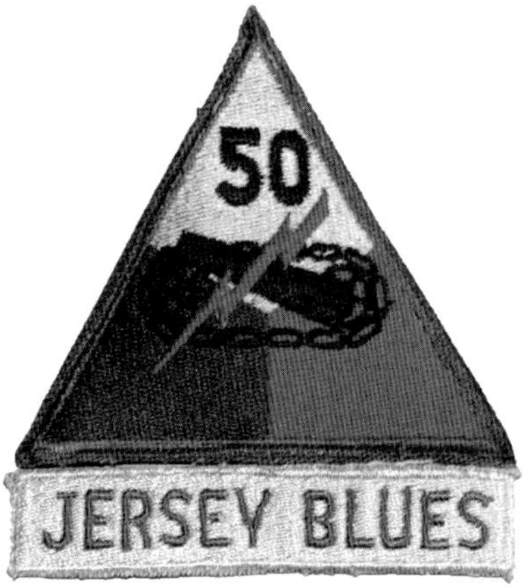

The Fiftieth Armored Division patch. *NGMMNJ.*

On April 18, Jackie Robinson, playing for the Montreal Royals in a season-opening AAA minor league game against the Jersey City Giants, broke baseball's "color line" at Jersey City's Roosevelt Stadium.

African American George Ashby, a sergeant in the Forty-fifth United States Colored Infantry during the Civil War, died at his home in Allentown on April 26. Ashby was the last surviving New Jersey Civil War veteran.

In July, the postwar New Jersey National Guard began to rebuild itself within a new division, the Fiftieth Armored Division. The Fiftieth's component units carried on the heritage and lineage of the old Forty-fourth Division of the prewar National Guard.

The Newark Eagles baseball team, one of the city's most visible and best-remembered African American business and entertainment institutions, reached the pinnacle of its success by defeating the Kansas City Monarchs and winning the Negro League World Championship.

New Jersey reached a total of one million telephones in service.

Newark airport was bustling, processing over one thousand passengers and one thousand tons of mail daily.

# 1947

Alfred E. Driscoll, the last governor elected under the constitution of 1844, was inaugurated on January 21. Driscoll was also the first governor elected under the new constitution of 1947, serving a three-year term and then a subsequent consecutive four-year term.

On June 25, the seven Weeks brothers—Robert, Edward, Albert, John, LeRoy, James and Joseph of Jersey City—showed up to enlist in the 309th Anti-Aircraft Artillery Battery of the New Jersey National Guard's 50th Armored Division. All but Joseph, who turned out to be an underage fifteen years old, were sworn into the organization, in the largest family military enlistment in New Jersey history.

In July, Lawrence "Larry" Doby of Paterson, a World War II navy veteran and star second baseman of the Newark Eagles of the Negro Baseball League, became the second African American to play in major-league baseball, when he was called up by the Cleveland Indians.

On December 23, John Bardeen and Walter Brattain of AT&T Bell Labs in Murray Hill, New Jersey, introduced the transistor, short for trans-resistance, which would replace tubes in radios.

The greatest twenty-four-hour snowfall recorded in New Jersey history occurred in Long Branch, Monmouth County, over December 26–27.

The Educational Testing Service, which would administer the college Scholastic Aptitude Test, among others, was founded in Princeton.

# 1948

On January 1, New Jersey adopted the new state constitution of 1947, approved by the voters the previous November, to replace the constitution of 1844, which, in its turn, had replaced the constitution of 1776. The office of the governor gained considerable power, and the incumbent was now allowed to serve two consecutive terms of four years each rather than the previous non-successive three-year terms.

On January 8, Governor Driscoll wrote to Secretary of Defense James V. Forrestal, advising him that the new constitution of New Jersey provided that "no person shall be discriminated against in the exercise of any civil or military right" and questioning army policy as enunciated in 1946, stating that African Americans could only serve in "Negro regiments or groups." In further correspondence, the governor told the secretary that New Jersey was desegregating its National Guard, and after initially threatening to withhold federal aid, the secretary allowed the state to proceed. New Jersey was the first state to desegregate its military.

On January 13, Fort Dix Army Air Base was renamed McGuire Air Force Base in honor of Thomas Buchanan McGuire, a Medal of Honor recipient and World War II ace from Ridgewood who died in a plane crash in the Philippines in 1945.

On June 3, Wall Township airport operator Ed Brown announced a combination drive-in/fly-in movie theater. Small planes could land on his adjacent runway and be towed the short distance back and forth to the outdoor theater.

On September 6, World War II veteran Harold Unruh killed thirteen men, women and children in Camden in a random shooting spree. Unruh was pronounced insane and spent the rest of his life in Trenton Psychiatric Hospital, dying there in 2009.

The New Jersey Turnpike Authority was created to supervise the building of the turnpike.

## 1949

Iconic New Jersey rock-and-roll musician Bruce Springsteen was born in Long Branch on September 29. Although New Jersey has produced many entertainers over the years, none is more associated with the state through his lyrics and themes than Springsteen.

June was the state's driest month on record, resulting in heavy crop damage. Yields of early sweet corn and early commercial potatoes were reduced by more than 50 percent. Pastures were brown, and dairy production greatly diminished.

On July 26, the U.S. Navy commissioned the USS *Basilone*, named in honor of John Basilone, the World War II hero Marine Corps sergeant from Raritan.

New Jersey established a state temporary disability insurance benefit plan for public and private workers.

In response to a service station in Hackensack that attracted customers by promising them a discount for pumping their own gasoline, the New Jersey Gasoline Retailers Association successfully lobbied for a law banning self-service at all gas stations in New Jersey. That law is still in force.

# 1950

The census reported New Jersey's population as 4,835,329.

On June 25, North Korea invaded South Korea, beginning the Korean War. More than 190,000 New Jerseyans served in the U.S. military during the Korean War between 1950 and its end in 1953, and 836 lost their lives. New Jerseyans Nelson V. Brittin of Audubon, Hector A. Cafferata of Montville and Samuel F. Coursen of Madison were awarded the Congressional Medal of Honor for their heroism during the conflict.

During the Korean War, the New Jersey Air National Guard's 108th Fighter Wing, 108th Fighter Group, 141st Fighter Squadron, 108th Air Base Group, 108th Maintenance and Supply Group, 108th Medical Group, 141st Weather Station and 105th Aircraft Control and Warning Squadron were activated. None of these units was deployed in Korea, however. Army National Guard units called up during the Korean War included the 112th Artillery Group Headquarters, 695th Armored Field Artillery Battalion, 30th Ordnance Battalion, 122nd Ordnance Company, 63rd Army Band and the 150th Engineer Pontoon Bridge Company. As with the Air National Guard units, none was deployed in Korea.

Chapter 7

# 1951 to 2014

## 1951

On February 6, the crowded Pennsylvania Railroad train No. 733, known as the "Broker" due to the preponderance of Wall Street executives aboard, careened from the rails in Woodbridge and hurtled down a forty-foot embankment. The accident killed eighty-four commuters and one crew member in one of the worst rail disasters in New Jersey or United States history.

On November 10, the first coast-to-coast direct dial telephone call was made by Mayor M. Leslie Denning of Englewood, who called the mayor of Alameda, California.

The first fifty-three-mile section of the New Jersey Turnpike was opened between Deepwater and Bordentown in November. Other sections were opened over the next few months.

The Molly Pitcher Handicap at Monmouth Park became the first horse race televised in color.

A party was held at Laird & Company in Monmouth County when the millionth case of Laird's apple brandy produced since the repeal of the Eighteenth Amendment was packed. Every employee received a silver dollar for each year of his or her employment.

Arnold Raymond Cream of Pennsauken, better known as Jersey Joe Walcott, became the world's heavyweight champion at the relatively advanced age of thirty-seven on July 18.

A group of Gibbstown boys claimed to have seen a monster resembling the legendary Jersey Devil. Descriptions of the strange visitor ranged from a chunky man with a bestial face to a half-man, half-beast creature. Responding to the concerns of alarmed townspeople, authorities conducted a search with floodlights—to no avail. The police chief, frustrated by an avalanche of inquiries, placed signs on the outskirts of town asserting that the Jersey Devil was a hoax, in an effort to discourage flocks of tourists.

## 1952

The final stretch of the New Jersey Turnpike, between Newark and Ridgefield Park, was opened in January. The turnpike, extending from the Delaware Memorial Bridge to the George Washington Bridge, took only twenty-three months to construct.

## 1953

Republican senator Joseph R. McCarthy began his investigation of "Communist subversion" at Fort Monmouth, headquarters of the U.S. Army Signal Corps, charging that Soviet agents had penetrated the base and stolen highly classified information. In response, the army suspended forty-two scientists, engineers and technicians who worked there.

## 1954

On October 23, opening ceremonies were held for the Garden State Parkway, although the original 164 miles of the road were not completed until 1956. A 9-mile extension was added to the parkway to connect it to the New York Thruway in 1957.

The amazing twelve-month, round-the-world journey of sixty-two-year-old Marion Hart came to a conclusion at Teterboro Airport on July 11. Having learned to fly at age fifty-four at Teterboro, Hart flew her single-engine Beechcraft Bonanza thirty-five thousand miles to twenty-five countries.

*On the Waterfront*, a Columbia Pictures production starring a brooding young Marlon Brando, opened. Filmed in Hoboken and based on actual events that took place on the docks, the film would win eight Oscars.

## 1955

As a result of a seven-year campaign by the New Jersey State Federation of Women's Clubs, the New Jersey College for Women, a college of Rutgers University, was renamed Douglass College, in honor of founder and first dean Mabel Smith Douglass.

## 1956

The U.S. Military Assistance Advisory Group (MAAG) assumed responsibility from the French for training South Vietnamese military forces.

A June 10 hailstorm wreaked havoc in Hunterdon and Warren Counties, causing extensive damage to crops, houses, trees and automobiles. Hailstones varying in size from mothballs to golf balls were sighted and, in some places, piled four to five inches high.

Camp Kilmer, which had been deactivated in 1949 and then reopened shortly afterward, acted as a reception center for thirty thousand Hungarian refugees who fled their country after the Soviet Union suppressed the Hungarian revolution.

The Hudson County extension of the New Jersey Turnpike between Newark Airport and Jersey City was completed, as was a six-mile direct connection with the Pennsylvania Turnpike.

Transistor inventors John Bardeen and Walter Brattain of AT&T Bell Labs in Murray Hill, New Jersey, along with William Schockley, who improved the transistor, were awarded a Nobel Prize.

## 1957

Advertising man James Vicary allegedly secretly used the Lee Theatre in Fort Lee to test subliminal message advertising during a film, although the extent of the testing or even whether the experiment was actually carried out are a matter of dispute.

The first New Jersey state Little League championship was played.

## 1958

On September 15, a Central Railroad of New Jersey morning commuter train derailed and slid off the Newark Bay lift bridge in Bayonne. Both diesel locomotives and the first two coaches plunged into Newark Bay and sank, immediately killing forty-eight people.

A reorganization of the Army National Guard integrated its mission with that of the regular army. The New Jersey Army National Guard organized Nike Hercules air defense missile batteries for the defense of the New York Metropolitan area that were manned around the clock and fully integrated

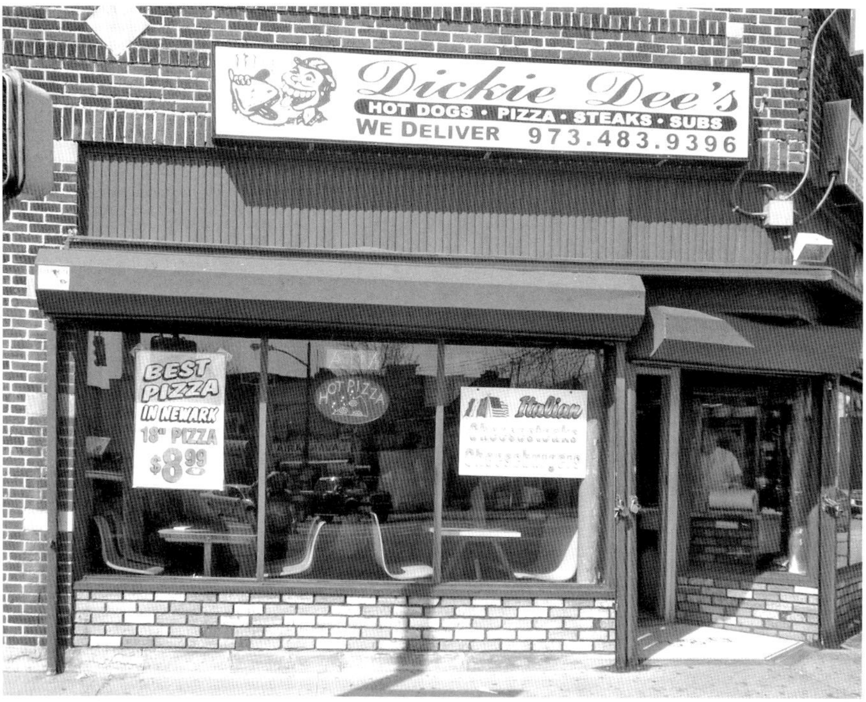


Dickie Dee's Italian Hot Dog Emporium opened in 1958 and is still going strong in Newark. *Joseph G. Bilby.*

into the national air defense system. The 1st Battalion, 254th Air Defense Artillery, the unit charged with this responsibility, was inactivated in 1974.

Dominic D'Innocenzio (Dickie Dee) and Enrico Bruno founded "Dickie Dee's" Italian hot dog eatery on lower Bloomfield Avenue in Newark. It still stands today, a classic Jersey joint now run by Dominic's son Rick D'Innocenzio, a former baseball standout at St. Benedict's Preparatory School in Newark and the University of Miami. There are disputes among aficionados as to whether Dickie Dee's or Jimmy Buff's makes the best true original-style Italian hot dog, but both rate highly.

## 1959

On February 27, Newark-born gangster Abner "Longy" Zwillman, who had been subpoenaed to appear before a U.S. Senate Committee investigating organized crime, was found hanged in his West Orange home. Zwillman's death was ruled a suicide, although many thought he was killed on the orders of other organized crime figures.

On July 21, the first atomic-powered merchant ship, the SS *Savannah*, was christened at Camden.

The "Jersey Barrier," a highway divider developed by Stevens Institute of Technology at the request of the New Jersey Highway Department, was formally introduced.

A regional maintenance and support facility for Nike antiaircraft missile batteries deployed in defense of the New York metropolitan area was established at Camp Kilmer.

## 1960

The United States census reported New Jersey's population as 6,066,782.

The Great Swamp National Wildlife Refuge was established near Morristown, saving an environmentally sensitive area of marshes, swamps, ponds, streams, woodlands and wildlife from the possibility of being destroyed to construct an airport.

On August 21, John Brodeur, an accountant from Jersey City, was visiting his fiancée, a Jersey City teacher working at the Stockton Hotel in Sea Girt for the summer. Brodeur swam out from the hotel employees' beach to body surf a wave and was attacked by a shark. Rushed to Jersey Shore Hospital in Neptune for emergency surgery, Brodeur lost his leg below the knee. It was the first documented shark attack on a New Jersey beach since 1916, although there had been incidents involving sharks off the New Jersey coast. On August 26, two entrepreneurs from Orange came to Sea Girt peddling a proposed shark proof "bubble fence." Testing proved the device to be totally ineffective.

On August 22, a fourteen-year-old boy was attacked by a shark in the surf at Seaside Park. His knee was ripped to the bone, but his leg was saved.

## 1961

A significant maritime disaster occurred on January 15, when twenty-eight U.S. Air Force officers and men manning Texas Tower #4, a Distant Early Warning (DEW) radar station platform located fifty-eight miles off the New Jersey coast due east of Belmar, were lost at sea when the tower collapsed during a winter storm. Only two bodies were ever found.

James Joseph Gandolfini Jr. was born on September 18 in Westwood. Gandolfini would become an actor and gain fame for his role as New Jersey

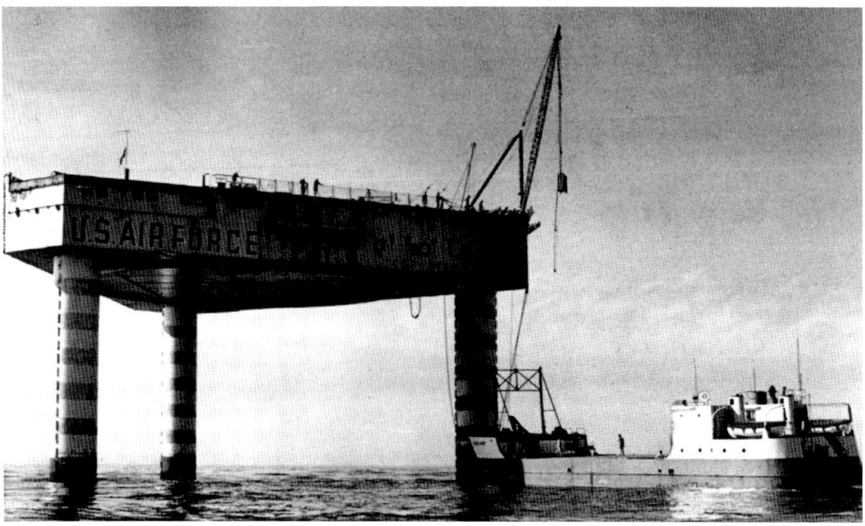


After the disaster with Texas Tower #4, the remaining towers were gradually demolished. This is Tower #5, its superstructure removed, awaiting demolition. *Joseph G. Bilby.*

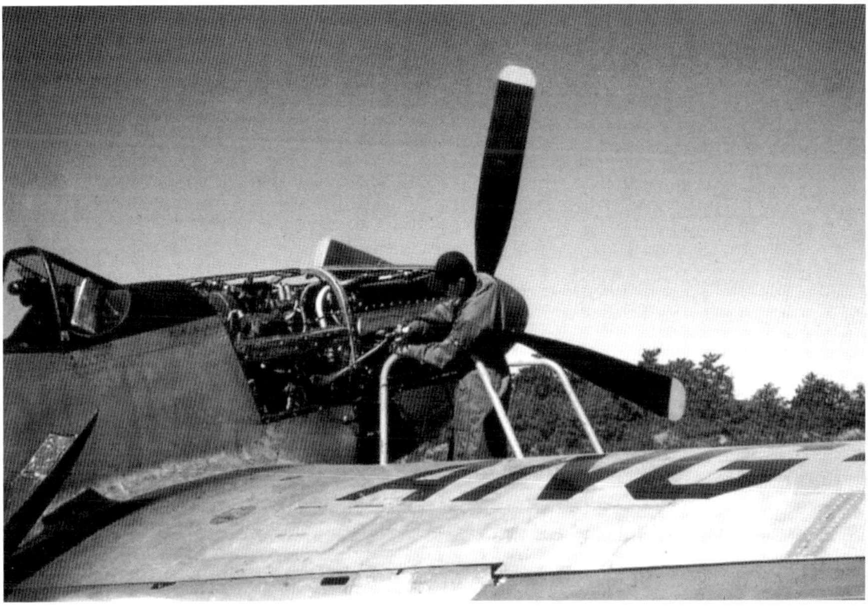

New Jersey Air National Guardsmen of the 108th Tactical Fighter Wing deployed to France during the Berlin Crisis of 1961. *NGMMNJ*.

Mafia boss Tony Soprano in the HBO series *The Sopranos*, which ran from 1999 to 2007 for a total of eighty-six episodes. Gandolfini died on June 19, 2013.

During the Berlin Crisis of October 1961, the New Jersey Air National Guard's 108th Tactical Fighter Wing and its support squadrons were deployed to Chaumont, France, to augment NATO forces. The 112th Artillery Group Headquarters, 30th Ordnance Battalion, 122nd Ordnance Company, 114th Surgical Hospital, 141st and 253rd Transportation Companies of the New Jersey Army National Guard reported to stateside posts for federal duty.

The first enclosed, climate-controlled mall on the East Coast opened in Cherry Hill on the former site of a sixteen-acre farm. The opulent shopping center featured ninety stores, exotic birds, tropical plants, fountains and a movie theater.

## 1962

The great storm of March 6 through March 8 brought snow, sleet, wind and tides ten feet above normal to the Jersey Shore. Before the winds and tides abated, millions of tons of sand were shifted, shorelines changed and new inlets were carved across the narrow, sandy barrier islands off the coast. Long Beach Island was hit particularly hard, with communities such as Harvey Cedars and Loveladies completely cut off from the outside world.

Freddy Cannon's song "Palisades Park" brought Palisades Amusement Park, a thirty-eight-acre amusement center on top of the Palisades cliffs in Bergen County, to international prominence. The song, with its catchphrase "Come on over," reached number three on the U.S. charts and number 20 in Great Britain.

Newark's Frankie Valli and the Four Seasons recorded "Sherry," beginning their reign at the top of the pop charts.

## 1963

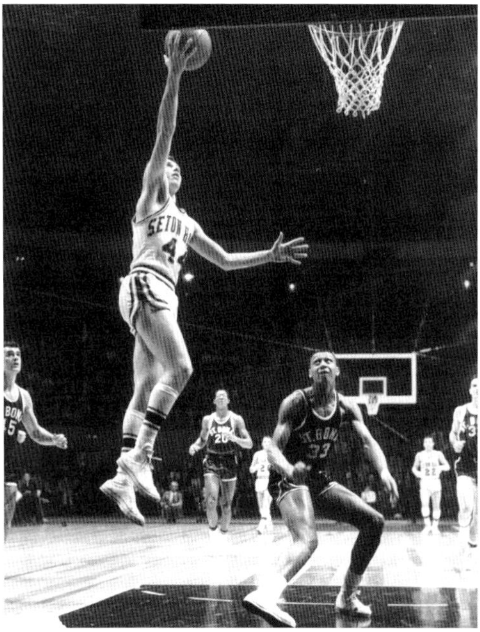

Seton Hall University's Nick Werkman was national collegiate basketball scoring champion in 1963. *Seton Hall University Athletic Department.*

Basketball player Nick Werkman of Seton Hall University won the national scoring title with an average of 29.5 points per game. Werkman was also named to several all-America teams that year.

State land acquisition began at the site of the Revolutionary War Battle of Monmouth Court House site under the "Green Acres Program."

The largest wildfire in the Pinelands' recorded history burned nearly 190,000 acres of Pinelands, destroying 185 homes and killing seven people.

Snowboarding pioneer Tom Sims of Haddonfield created the "ski board," an early version of the snowboard.

## 1964

On December 19, the first indoor collegiate football game was played in Atlantic City, pitting the University of West Virginia against the University of Utah.

Kathryn Elkus White of Red Bank was appointed the U.S. ambassador to Denmark. Her father, Abram I. Elkus, was ambassador to Turkey during the Woodrow Wilson administration.

Teaneck was the first community in the country to voluntarily integrate its schools.

## 1965

At an April 23 anti–Vietnam War "teach in" at Rutgers University, Professor Eugene Genovese said, "Those of you who know me know that I am a Marxist and a socialist. Therefore, unlike some of my distinguished colleagues here this morning, I do not fear or regret the impending Viet Cong victory in Vietnam. I welcome it." His words became a campaign issue with Democratic governor Richard Hughes defending Genovese's First Amendment right to say what he said, without endorsing his view, and his Republican opponent Wayne Dumont claiming that supporting the enemy was not appropriate for a professor at a taxpayer-funded state university. Hughes won the election, but Genovese, unhappy with Rutgers, moved on to Sir George Williams College in Montreal in 1967.

The first American combat troops, the Ninth Marine Expeditionary Brigade, arrived in Vietnam to defend the U.S. airfield at Danang.

Mildred Barry Hughes was the first woman elected to the New Jersey State Senate.

African American tennis great Althea Gibson moved to East Orange, where she became manager of the town's Department of Recreation. She was later named New Jersey State athletic director.

## 1966

The Jersey Devil was proposed as a subject for a U.S. postage stamp. The post office declined the proposal.

On February 25, marine staff sergeant Peter S. Connor of South Orange was mortally wounded in Vietnam, falling on a defective hand grenade to save his men from injury. His self-sacrifice was posthumously recognized when he was awarded the Medal of Honor for his heroism.

On October 6, Reverend Martin Luther King Jr. spoke to a crowded gymnasium at Monmouth College, West Long Branch. King said the nation had come a "long, long way" in dealing with racial injustice but cautioned there was a "long, long way to go" in effectively addressing the problem.

## 1967

For six days, from July 12 to July 17, Newark was rocked by a riot initially caused by the arrest of an African American taxi driver on motor vehicle violations. Protests grew out of frustration over numerous issues,

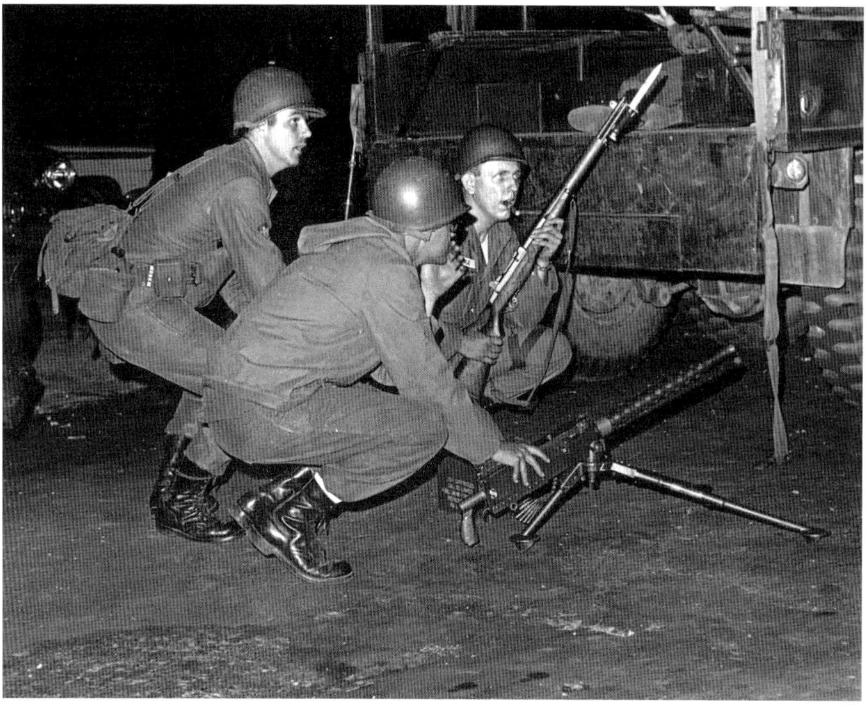

National Guardsmen were called into Newark during the civil disturbances there in July 1967. *NGMMNJ.*

including substandard housing, unemployment, alleged police brutality and inferior educational opportunities. Before the disturbances ended, the state police and the New Jersey Army National Guard had been called into the city. The riots killed twenty-six people and caused an estimated $10 million in damage.

In July, Maxine Hartman Nellen became the first woman to jump out of a hot-air balloon for her thousandth free-fall parachute jump over Lumberton.

On March 21, Ramsey-born U.S. Army master sergeant Charles Hosking of the Fifth Special Forces Group was mortally wounded during an operation to capture a Viet Cong sniper. The enemy soldier pulled the pin on a hand grenade, and Hosking grabbed him, taking the full force of the blast and saving his comrades. He was posthumously awarded the Medal of Honor for his heroism.

On June 23, President Lyndon B. Johnson and Soviet premier Aleksei Kosygin held the first of two summit meetings at Glassboro State College.

On September 21, U.S. Marine lance corporal Colby Barker of Park Ridge threw himself on a hand grenade to save his comrades in Vietnam. Barker was posthumously awarded the Medal of Honor for his heroic conduct.

On November 19, U.S. Army chaplain Major Charles J. Watters of Jersey City, a Seton Hall University graduate and Catholic priest, was killed by "friendly fire" when a mistakenly dropped American bomb landed on his position near Dak To, Vietnam. Immediately prior to his death, Watters, who was assigned to the 173rd Airborne Brigade, had repeatedly risked his life retrieving wounded men under enemy fire and was posthumously awarded the Medal of Honor.

In a landmark gay rights decision, the state Supreme Court reversed a local court ruling that allowed the Alcoholic Beverage Commission to close down Manny's Den, a New Brunswick bar, for allowing the "congregation of homosexuals."

The Newark Boys' Chorus School was founded in Newark. The chorus has performed to accolades around the world, and more than 90 percent of the school's graduates have gone on to college.

The New York Shipbuilding Corporation, a major employer in Camden County, closed its Camden shipyard after operating there since 1899.

# 1968

On February 19, U.S. Army staff sergeant Fred Zabitosky of Trenton, while wounded himself on a mission in Laos, rescued a helicopter pilot whose helicopter had crashed and was under heavy fire. He was awarded the Medal of Honor for his heroism.

On March 9, Woodbridge High School and Rutgers ROTC graduate first lieutenant Jack Jacobs, acting as an advisor to a South Vietnamese infantry unit, helped save fourteen American and Vietnamese soldiers who were under heavy enemy fire. Jacobs was awarded the Medal of Honor for his actions that day.

On September 6, feminist protestors held a demonstration outside the Miss America pageant in Atlantic City, tossing cosmetics, girdles and bras into a trash can, ostensibly for burning, although nothing was actually set afire.

The Garden State Arts Center, a seven-thousand-seat theater under a circular roof, with lawn seating for an additional 10,500 people, opened on the Garden State Parkway in Monmouth County. It has been a venue for popular entertainers, the New Jersey Symphony Orchestra, the New Jersey State Opera and the New Jersey Ballet, as well as other events, ever since. In 1996, the center, owned by the New Jersey Highway Authority, changed its name to the PNC Bank Arts Center due to bank sponsorship.

Tom and Margaret Potter opened the Upstage Club in Asbury Park, which became a showcase for promising young musicians, such as Bruce Springsteen and his earliest band mates, drummer Vini Lopez and guitarist Steve Van Zandt.

The USS *New Jersey* went into service off the coast of North Vietnam on September 29.

Princeton University admitted its first female undergraduates.

# 1969

Richard Stockton College of New Jersey, named after one of the New Jersey signers of the Declaration of Independence, was founded. The current campus is in the Pinelands in Pomona, but the first classes were held in the Mayflower Hotel in Atlantic City.

The 117th Tactical Fighter Group and the 119th Tactical Fighter Squadron of the New Jersey Air National Guard were ordered to active federal duty in

1969 following North Korean seizure of the USS *Pueblo*. Although the units were not deployed overseas, some group personnel were subsequently assigned to installations throughout Southeast Asia, Korea and the United States, and some pilots and other airmen joined combat units in South Vietnam.

In December, the Oyster Creek nuclear power plant in Ocean County was completed. It used water from two rivers in a system of cooling that discharged slightly warmer water into a canal connected to Barnegat Bay.

The New Jersey state lottery was approved to raise money for state government funding for education.

Astronaut Edwin "Buzz" Aldrin of Glen Ridge landed on the moon with Neil Armstrong.

Millicent Fenwick was first elected to the state assembly. She would go on to become a congresswoman and served as a model for the Lacy Davenport character in the comic strip *Doonesbury*.

## 1970

The United States census reported New Jersey's population as 7,171,112.

Two formerly traditional farm areas—Woodbridge and Clifton—emerged as New Jersey's seventh- and eighth-largest cities.

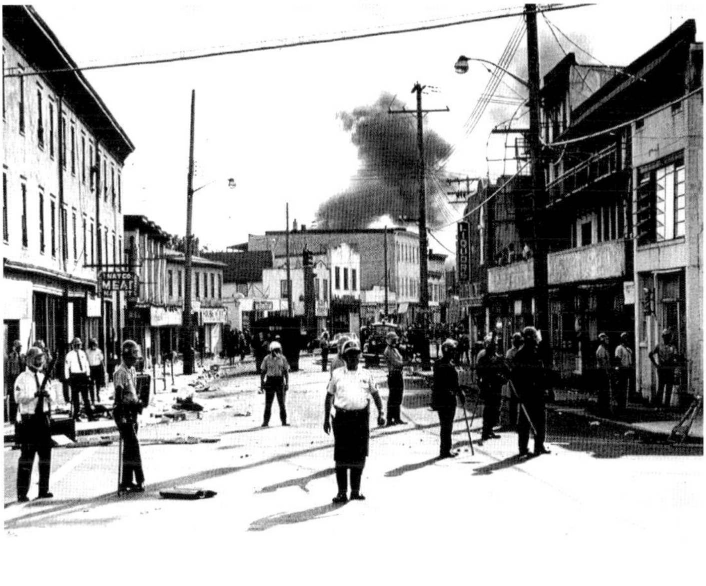

Springwood Avenue in Asbury Park during the civil disturbances in the city in 1970. *Joseph G. Bilby.*

Conservationists enjoyed their biggest victory to date when the New Jersey legislature created a Department of Environmental Protection. The new department focused attention on matters that two decades earlier were dismissed as being of concern only to "nature lovers" or bird watchers.

In November, Kenneth Gibson, a civil engineer, was elected as the first African American mayor of Newark. His predecessor, Hugh Addonizio, was convicted on extortion and conspiracy charges.

Reflecting the anger of African Americans frustrated with their lack of social and economic progress, riots broke out along Asbury Park's Springwood Avenue. The disturbances subsided within several days, leaving 180 people injured, 167 arrested and $4 million in property damage.

## 1971

Mild-mannered accountant John List of Westfield murdered his wife, three children and mother on November 9 and then left their bodies in the family's rambling Victorian home and disappeared for seventeen years. The bodies were not discovered for another month, after a neighbor noticed the house lights burning out. List was eventually found in Virginia, remarried and living under the name of Robert Clark, after a viewer recognized him from a segment on the TV show *America's Most Wanted*. List's excuse for murdering his family was that he wished to expedite their entry into heaven. List died in 2008 while serving a life term in Trenton State Prison.

## 1972

On August 31, the *Newark News* printed its last issue. Owned for generations by the Scudder family, the paper was sold to Media General of Richmond, Virginia, in the late 1960s, and the new company's incredibly incompetent management destroyed what had been the greatest newspaper ever published in New Jersey in a few short years.

Construction began on the Meadowlands Sports Complex.

The vote in New Jersey was extended to eighteen-year-olds.

Rutgers University became coeducational.

## 1973

A cease-fire agreement that, in the words of President Richard Nixon, "brings peace with honor in Vietnam and Southeast Asia" was signed in Paris by Henry Kissinger and Le Duc Tho. The agreement went into effect on January 28.

Historic Cold Spring Village, an outdoor living history museum, was founded in Cape May. The village is dedicated to preserving and interpreting the rural South Jersey community life of the mid-nineteenth century.

## 1974

The New Jersey Supreme Court declared that Little League Baseball Incorporated was a public rather than a private accommodation and could not discriminate against girls who wanted to join previously all-boy teams.

Asbury Park's Mayfair Theater, the majestic 1920s movie palace that epitomized the heyday of silent and early talking motion pictures, was razed, despite the efforts of preservationists to save it.

## 1975

The Vietnam War ended with the fall of Saigon on April 30. During the course of the war, 1,561 New Jersey men and one woman were listed as killed or missing in action.

On August 25, Bruce Springsteen's major hit "Born to Run" was released.

Lakewood's Little League baseball team defeated Tampa, Florida, four to three, winning the National Tournament of Champions.

## 1976

On September 1, the New Jersey Meadowlands racetrack opened.

On October 10, Giants' Stadium opened in the Meadowlands with a National Football League game between the Giants and Dallas Cowboys.

Centenary College for Women was established in Hackettstown, evolving out of Centenary Junior College, founded in 1940. The college became coeducational in 1988.

The New Jersey Supreme Court ruled that every school district in New Jersey had to provide a "thorough and efficient" education and ordered state government to help hard-pressed local school boards obtain the necessary funds for the program.

New Jersey initiated a state income tax.

Liberty State Park, a 1,200-acre tract next to Jersey City, opened on Flag Day, June 17. Among its attractions are a 36-acre natural area of marshes and a two-mile-long waterfront promenade.

New Jersey legalized privately owned gambling casinos, limited to Atlantic City, with tax revenue from these establishments earmarked to support education, the aged and the poor.

The New Jersey Supreme Court held that Karen Ann Quinlan, a twenty-two-year-old woman who lay in a coma and lacked all cognitive function, had the right to be disconnected from a respirator and that this right could be exercised by her father. Quinlan's was a landmark case because it established for the first time that incompetent individuals had the right to terminate life-sustaining medical treatment and that someone other than the patient could exercise this right.

## 1977

A massive fire destroyed Garden State Racetrack in Cherry Hill on April 14.

## 1978

On Saturday, May 27, Resorts International, the first gambling casino in Atlantic City, opened for business.

In June, Monmouth Battlefield State Park formally opened with a 200th anniversary reenactment of the battle.

Crossroads Theater in New Brunswick, the nation's leading African American theater, was founded by Ricardo Khan and L. Kenneth Richardson. The theater produced and toured new works from the

African diaspora and displayed positive images of African American life, history and culture.

Preservation New Jersey was founded. It is a nonprofit organization promoting historic resources, communities and landscapes around the state of New Jersey.

## 1979

New Jersey Transit was created as a division of the New Jersey Department of Transportation. In 1983, it took over the commuter rail lines being abandoned by bankrupt commercial railroads in the state. Running both railroad and bus lines, New Jersey Transit carried an average of 103,000 rail passengers and 255,000 bus passengers to and from work each day in 2001.

Italian American Genovese crime family figure Anthony "Little Pussy" Russo was shot to death by fellow Genovese mob members on April 26 in Long Branch while on an Easter furlough from prison.

The Pinelands Preservation Act was passed, providing for environmental protection and limited development in a vast stretch of southern New Jersey.

## 1980

The census bureau reported New Jersey's population as 7.4 million, almost double the pre–World War II total.

On April 21, ironically the tenth anniversary of Earth Day, over ten thousand drums of highly toxic chemicals caught fire at the site of the Chemical Control Company in Elizabeth. Toxins filled the air, and the Elizabeth River turned red. In the aftermath, the officers of the company were prosecuted, convicted and sentenced to jail. The New Jersey Department of Environmental Protection cleaned up the immediate damage on the site and introduced long-term remediation measures to complete the job.

On October 30, New Jersey Democratic senator Harrison Williams was indicted in the "Abscam" sting operation in which an FBI informant posed as a Middle Eastern sheik and offered bribes to a number of politicians in return for political favors. Williams was convicted in 1981 and, still protesting his innocence, resigned from the senate in 1982 when threatened with expulsion. He served time in prison for the offense.

## 1981

The Education Law Center filed a complaint in Superior Court on behalf of twenty children attending public schools in Camden, East Orange, Irvington and Jersey City. The lawsuit, which challenged New Jersey's system of financing public education, was the first salvo in the historic case of *Abbott v. Burke*, widely recognized as groundbreaking litigation on behalf of poor and minority schoolchildren. The results, with more money expended in poor districts, have been mixed.

On July 2, Bruce Springsteen was the opening act for the Continental Airlines Arena, built as part of the Meadowlands Sports complex in East Rutherford.

## 1982

Anne Karas was brutally stabbed to death outside a movie theater in Long Branch's fashionable West End while spending a night out with her husband, Walter. Police arrested Mary Claire Williams, who said she conspired with her lover, Walter Karas, to murder his wife.

Governor Thomas Kean reinstated the death penalty for certain murders. No one has actually been executed between then and this writing, however.

On December 28, the USS *New Jersey* was re-commissioned once more, this time to serve in the Persian Gulf

A fire destroyed about one-third of the length of the Atlantic City Steel Pier.

Drumthwacket, a stately Greek Revival mansion in Princeton, became the official residence of the governor of New Jersey. It replaced Morven, which was built in the 1750s and initially served as the home of Richard Stockton, a signer of the Declaration of Independence, and his wife, Annis Boudinot Stockton, a published poet.

## 1983

The EPA added the Ciba-Geigy site in Dover Township to the Superfund National Priorities List because of harmful chemicals found in the soil and groundwater. The 1,400-acre site contained a facility that manufactured pigments, dyes, resins and epoxy. Sludge and processed carcinogenic waste had been disposed of on the site and seeped into the groundwater.

The New Jersey Supreme Court's Mount Laurel II ruling reaffirmed the Mount Laurel Doctrine, which called for the construction of "affordable housing" for low- and moderate-income households in otherwise more upscale and expensive communities.

## 1984

Eight teenage visitors were trapped and killed inside the Haunted Castle at Six Flags Great Adventure Park in Jackson after a fire broke out and destroyed the structure.

Bruce Springsteen released the iconic album *Born in the U.S.A.*

## 1985

On May 7, demolition began at Roosevelt Stadium in Jersey City, where Jackie Robinson broke the "color barrier," in order to make way for housing construction.

## 1986

On September 7, Maria Marshall, the wife of Robert O. Marshall of Toms River, was murdered by two men from Louisiana while he was allegedly unconscious at a Garden State Parkway picnic area in Lacey Township. After an investigation, the murderers were arrested, as was Marshall, who was accused of hiring them as contract killers. Marshall was convicted and sentenced to death, but his sentence was later changed to life in prison due to a judge's ruling that his attorney did not represent him effectively in the death sentence phase of the case. He is eligible for parole in 2014.

Sayreville native John Francis Bonjiovi, also known as Jon Bon Jovi, released his most successful album, *Slippery When Wet*, including such hits as "Livin' on a Prayer."

New Jersey began the cleanup of its Superfund pollution sites, the legacy of nineteenth- and twentieth-century unregulated industrialization, which, at the time, was welcomed as "progress."

Ferry service crossing the Hudson River between Weehawken and Thirty-eighth Street in Manhattan was reinstated after an absence of twenty-nine years.

## 1987

On June 8, a gas leak and electrical fire under the Long Branch pier destroyed the structure, a major New Jersey Shore venue that included a ten-thousand-square-foot haunted mansion and numerous other attractions.

The two remaining male-only eating clubs (Tiger Inn and Ivy Club) at Princeton University were ordered to admit women by the state's Division on Civil Rights based on a sex discrimination suit filed by Sally Frank in 1979.

## 1988

Donald Payne of Newark was elected as the state's first black congressman.

## 1989

A seventeen-year-old mentally handicapped girl was molested with a broomstick and baseball bat by members of the Glen Ridge High School football team. The event attracted national attention and was documented in a book and television movie.

# 1990

The United States census reported New Jersey's population as 7,730,188.

The stage, film and television actress Joan Bennett, who was born in Palisades Park, died on December 7. Bennett enjoyed a thriving movie career in the 1930s and 1940s, as well as a starring role in the 1960s television cult classic *Dark Shadows*.

# 1991

New Jersey's last drive-in movie theater, the Route 35 Drive-In in Hazlet, closed in September.

Three units of the New Jersey Army National Guard were mobilized for service in the Persian Gulf War of 1991, and one additional unit was mobilized for stateside service. In all, more than seven hundred New Jersey National Guard soldiers and airmen participated in support of Operation Desert Shield/Desert Storm.

The USS *New Jersey* was decommissioned for the final time on February 8.

# 1992

On September 25, a spacecraft built at General Electric's Astrospace Division in Princeton was launched at Cape Canaveral, Florida, in a multi-year odyssey to Mars. Developed and built by more than one thousand scientists and engineers in a huge satellite hangar, the 5,600-pound Mars Observer cost $511 million.

Fort Dix, which produced hundreds of thousands of soldiers during World Wars I and II, Korea, the Cold War and Vietnam, graduated its last class of basic trainees and closed as a regular army training base.

## 1993

Groundbreaking ceremonies took place in October for the New Jersey Performing Arts Center in downtown Newark, with performances by Kathleen Battle and the Newark Boys Chorus, among others. More than six million people have visited the center, one of the largest performing arts venues in the United States, since it opened in 1997.

Liberty Science Center, a museum at Liberty State Park in Jersey City dedicated to the exploration of nature, humanity and technology, opened its doors to visitors on January 24. By spring 1999, the museum welcomed its five-millionth guest, making it one of the Tristate region's most visited family attractions.

## 1994

Christine Todd Whitman was inaugurated as New Jersey's first female governor on January 18.

Megan's Law, designed to protect the public against sex offenders, was passed by the state legislature and signed by Governor Whitman. It was named after seven-year-old Megan Kanka, who was raped and murdered in Hamilton by Jesse Timmendequas, a neighbor with two prior convictions for sex offenses. The Kanka family was extremely active in lobbying for the legislation, which was enacted three months after Megan's death.

## 1995

The New Jersey Devils hockey team won the Stanley Cup, becoming the first professional sports champions in the state. They also won the cup in 2000 and 2003.

On May 7, the New Jersey Vietnam Veterans' Memorial, situated alongside the Garden State Parkway in Holmdel, was dedicated. The memorial, a circular open-air pavilion, is ringed with black granite panels, each representing a day of the year, engraved with the names of New Jerseyans who died on that day during the war. Three sculpted figures—a dying soldier, a nurse and a standing soldier—represent those who died, women who served and those who survived the conflict.

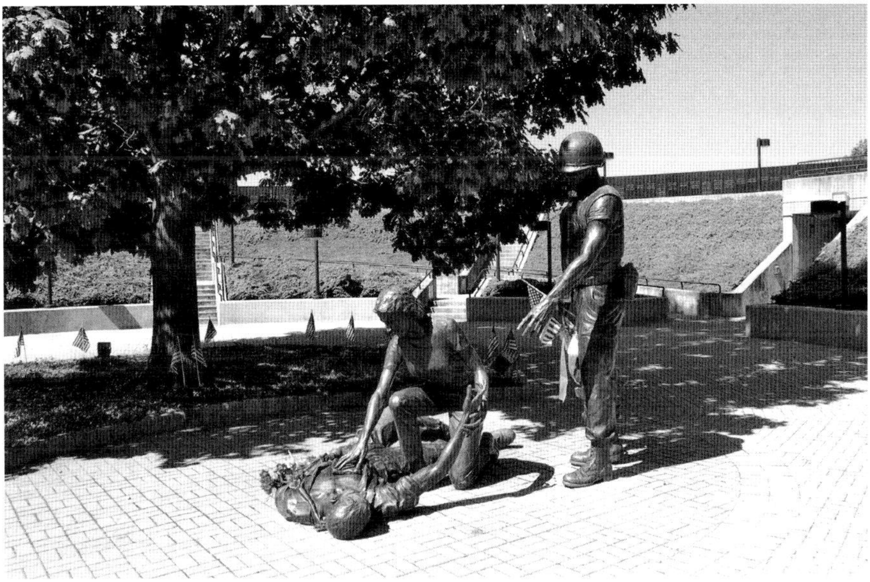

The New Jersey Vietnam Veterans' Memorial in Holmdel was dedicated in May 1995. *Joseph G. Bilby.*

## 1996

A major blizzard hit the Northeast, dumping thirty-seven inches of snow over parts of the state. At least one hundred deaths and $1 billion dollars in damage were reported across the region.

## 1997

The state removed regulations preventing same-sex couples from adopting children, making it the first to place gay and lesbian couples on an equal basis with heterosexual couples in the adoption process.

## 1998

The U.S. Supreme Court acknowledged New Jersey's sovereignty over the twenty-four and a half acres of Ellis Island created through federal landfill projects, while allowing New York sovereignty over the island's original three acres.

On August 27, the Toms River East American Little League team beat the South team from North Carolina, winning the U.S. Championship in the Little League World Series.

On September 27, the nation's first Vietnam War Museum opened as the Vietnam Era Educational Center, adjacent to the New Jersey Vietnam Veterans' Memorial.

## 1999

In April, two New Jersey state troopers were indicted on charges that they falsified police reports to disguise how they targeted African Americans for traffic stops and roadside drug searches. In announcing the indictments, the state attorney general reversed the official state position and conceded for the first time that some troopers had been stopping cars based solely on the race of the driver.

On May 7, the first of four thousand Kosovar refugees, ethnic Albanians from the disputed Serbian province of Kossovo, arrived at Fort Dix from camps in Macedonia prior to relocation around the country. The United States pledged to take in a total of twenty thousand Kosovar refugees.

Hurricane Floyd pounded the state with torrential rains and high winds. Several towns, including Bound Brook, South Bound Brook and Manville, were hard hit by record flooding.

## 2000

The United States census reported New Jersey's population as 8,414,350.

The New Jersey Korean War Memorial in Atlantic City was dedicated by Governor Whitman on November 13. Governor Whitman was named as head of the Environmental Protection Agency in President George W. Bush's administration.

A residence hall fire on January 19 at Seton Hall University killed three people and led to nationwide efforts to improve the safety of higher education dormitory facilities.

The Hudson-Bergen Light Rail service began operation from Bayonne. The rail system now extends to Weehawken.

## 2001

In the September 11 terrorist attack on the World Trade Center twin towers in New York City, 679 New Jerseyans died.

A commercial airplane flight that originated at Newark Airport was hijacked as part of the September 11 terrorist attack. The hijackers' plans to crash the plane in Washington, most likely into the United States Capitol building, were ruined when passengers attacked them, and the plane crashed. Everyone onboard died. One of the leaders among the passengers was New Jerseyan Todd Beamer of Plainsboro, whose words heard over a telephone—"Are you guys ready? Let's roll."—became a symbol of resistance to terrorism.

Shortly after the September 11 attack, F-16 fighter planes from the New Jersey Air National Guard's 177th Fighter Interceptor Group provided air cover over New York City and the eastern seaboard. Other Army and Air National Guard units quickly established a command post at Task Force Liberty headquarters at Liberty State Park and began security patrols at bridges, airports, tunnels and nuclear facilities. The New Jersey Army National Guard was also responsible for Task Force Respect, established at the Freshkills landfill on Staten Island, where debris from the World Trade Center was sifted and the remains of victims carefully collected.

The battleship USS *New Jersey* became a museum on the Camden waterfront.

Shirley M. Tilghman, a professor of molecular biology, was named the first female president of Princeton University.

## 2002

Many Asbury Park supporters were disgruntled when *City by the Sea*, a movie ostensibly set in a run-down Long Island city but filmed in Asbury Park, premiered. The gritty film featured the star power of Robert DeNiro, but what most local people remembered was its unflattering portrayal of their city. Set designers littered the boardwalk with debris and hired graffiti artists from the Bronx to create a seedy, threatening environment.

Former governor Thomas Kean was appointed to head the National Commission on Terrorist Attacks upon the United States (also known as the 9/11 Commission), an independent, bipartisan investigative working group created by congressional legislation and the signature of President George W. Bush to investigate the causes of the September 11, 2001 attacks and provide recommendations to prevent future terrorist attacks.

## 2003

In February, the 253rd Transportation Company, New Jersey National Guard, deployed to join the American forces preparing to invade Iraq.

Despite protests, New Jersey initiated its first bear hunt in thirty-three years. Hunters killed 323 bears.

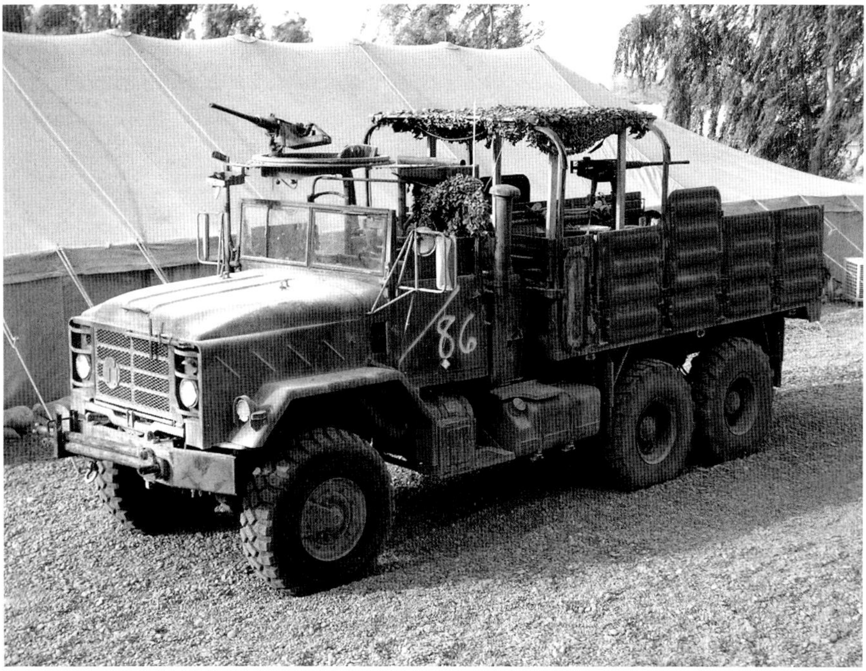


A convoy escort vehicle used by Cape May's 253rd Truck Company in Iraq in 2003. *NGMMNJ.*

## 2004

New Jersey National Guard support units, including signal corps, maintenance and finance detachments, were deployed to Iraq to supplement the Forty-second Division.

On August 12, Governor James E. McGreevey announced his resignation, disclosing that he was gay and had had an adulterous affair with another man. McGreevey said his decision to step down was prompted by concerns that the circumstances surrounding his affair would impair his ability to govern.

The Delsea Drive-in Theater in Vineland, which closed in 1987, reopened as the only drive-in theater in New Jersey.

## 2005

Pope John Paul celebrated Mass in Sacred Heart Cathedral in Newark.

More New Jersey National Guard support units were deployed to Iraq. The state's National Guard also provided support to Hurricane Katrina victims.

New Jersey was the first state to award public funding for stem-cell research.

In April, the General Motors auto assembly plant in Linden closed.

## 2006

On July 1, the New Jersey legislature failed to produce a budget, and Governor Jon S. Corzine threatened to close state government offices, beaches, parks and casinos amid a bitter dispute with fellow Democrats in the assembly over his plans to increase the sales tax. The governor and lawmakers reached a deal on a new budget on July 6, and on July 8, Corzine signed an executive order ending a weeklong shutdown.

## 2007

On February 17, the state recognized legal civil unions of same-sex couples.

Six men were arrested on charges of plotting to attack the Fort Dix army base. The men, all foreign-born and described as "Islamic militants," planned to use automatic weapons to kill as many soldiers as possible. They were tried, convicted and sentenced in 2008.

## 2008

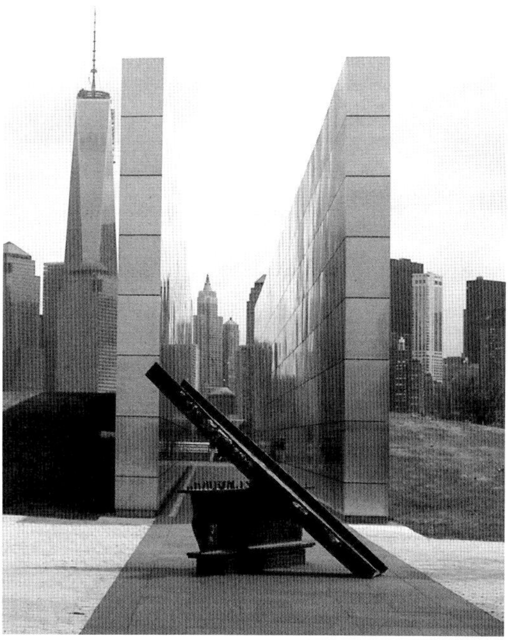

In 2008, a memorial to those New Jerseyans lost on September 11 was dedicated in Liberty State Park in Jersey City. *James M. Madden.*

In June, three thousand men and women of the Fiftieth Infantry Brigade Combat Team of the New Jersey Army National Guard left Fort Dix for Fort Bliss Texas for mobilization training and then left from there for nine months of service in Iraq.

On September 11, the "Empty Sky" memorial was dedicated in honor of the 679 New Jersey lives lost at the World Trade Center on September 11, 2001. The memorial, featuring thirty-foot-high twin brushed stainless steel walls with the victims' names inscribed on them, is located in Liberty State Park, Jersey City.

On November 11, Governor Jon Corzine and Adjutant General Major General Glenn K. Reith dedicated a memorial monument to New Jerseyans who served in the armed forces during World War II. The monument, located in Veterans' Park across from the statehouse, is a twelve-foot-high, one-ton bronze statue of "Lady Victory" atop a five-foot pedestal. More than 500,000 New Jerseyans served in World War II, and more than 30,000 made the ultimate sacrifice.

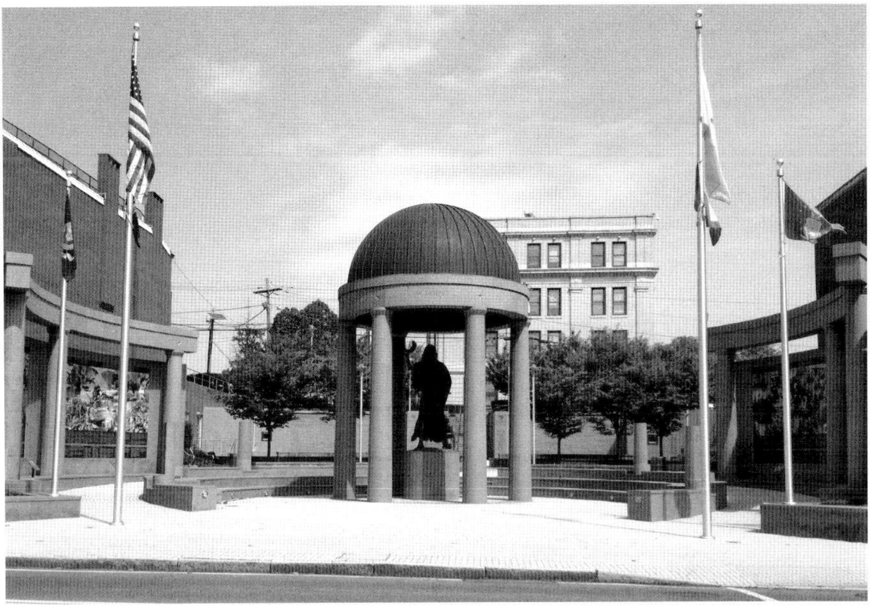

*Above*: In November 2008, Governor Corzine and Adjutant General Reith dedicated the New Jersey World War II Memorial in Trenton. *Geoffrey Jenkins.*

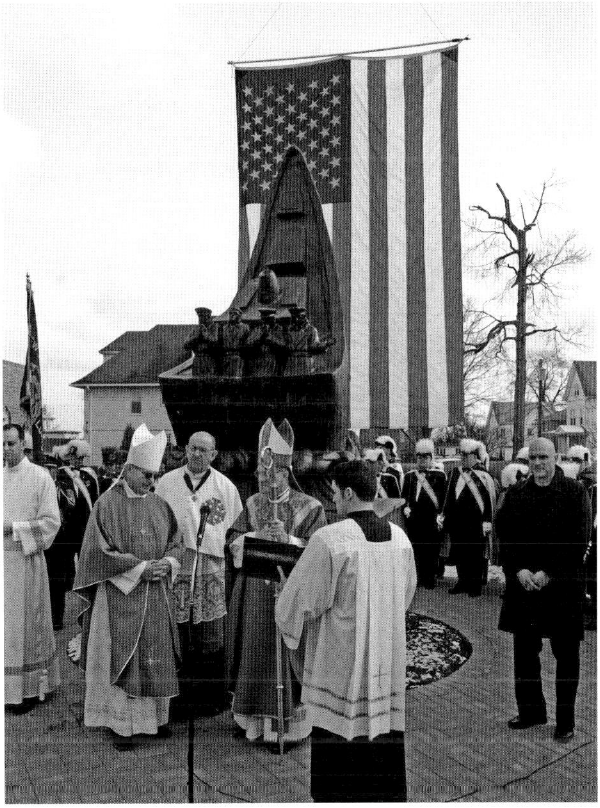

*Right*: The February 3, 2013 dedication of the memorial to the World War II Four Chaplains, including New Jersey's Father John Washington, in Kearny. *Photograph by Ed Civinskas.*

Despite the ardent efforts of preservationists, the Palace, a landmark amusement venue in Asbury Park, was demolished. The Palace complex began as a nineteenth-century Victorian structure that housed a merry-go-round and Ferris wheel and evolved into a sprawling expanse of funhouses, rides and games of chance. At night, the grinning neon countenance of Tillie, an impish clown, winked impudently at passersby.

## 2009

*Jersey Shore*, a reality TV series on the MTV network, debuted on December 3. The show, which followed a band of hard-partying housemates spending the summer in Seaside Heights, generated controversy over its alleged Italian American stereotyping and garnered record ratings for MTV.

## 2010

The United States census reported New Jersey's population as 8,791,898.

Tyler Clementi, an eighteen-year-old Rutgers University student, killed himself after discovering his roommate had secretly used a webcam to stream Clementi's romantic encounter with another man. Clementi jumped off the George Washington Bridge, and his suicide focused national attention on the victimization of gay, lesbian, bisexual and transgender youth.

The Jersey City Board of Education donated the statue of Pieter Stuyvesant, erected in 1913 on Bergen Avenue, to Hudson County Community College. The college intended to move the statue to a pocket park opposite its Culinary Arts Center, but the granite base was destroyed during the removal effort. The board subsequently discovered that it did not own the statue, the city did, and it ended up in a public works warehouse.

## 2011

The retreat call was sounded, and the American flag was lowered for the last time at Fort Monmouth. The U.S. Army installation that paved the way for communication technology in the military for ninety-four years was closed due to cost-cutting measures.

## 2012

On March 28, New Jersey governor Chris Christie dedicated a statue of Althea Gibson, the first black woman to win the Wimbledon Tennis Tournament, at the Althea Gibson Tennis Court Complex in Newark. Gibson died in East Orange in 2003 at age seventy-six and is buried in Rosedale Cemetery in Orange.

On June 3, more than three thousand people assembled to dedicate an eight-foot-high statue of major-league baseball player Roberto Clemente, who died in a plane crash on December 31, 1972, while delivering aid to victims of an earthquake in Nicaragua. Admirer Louis Lopez, founder of Newark's Roberto Clemente Little League in 1977, joined forces with Essex

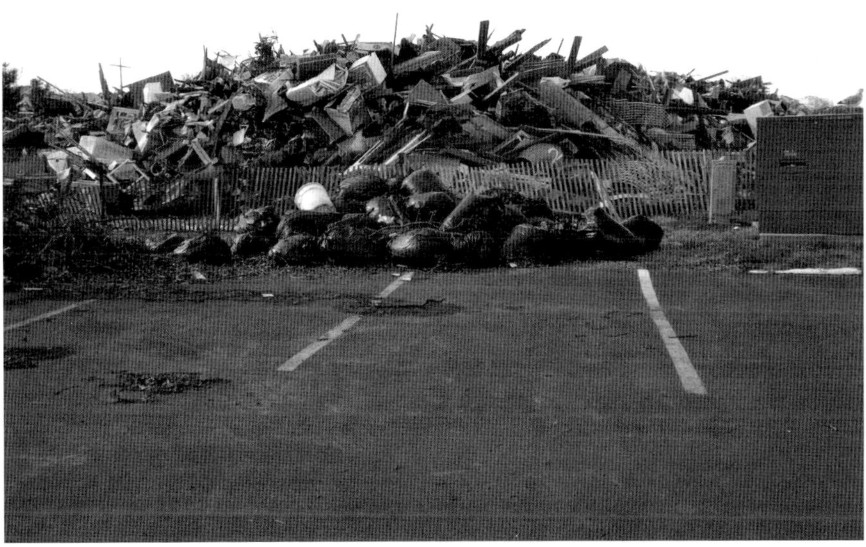

A mountain of debris from ruined homes in Belmar was piled in the marina parking lot for disposal after Hurricane Sandy. *Joseph G. Bilby.*

County Executive Joe DiVincenzo, a fellow Little League organizer and Clemente fan, to raise the $110,000 to pay for the statue.

On October 29, Hurricane Sandy crash-landed on the coast near Atlantic City, producing an unrelenting storm surge that devastated the Jersey Shore, destroying homes and businesses and damaging or destroying protective dunes. Nearly three million people lost power, many for more than two weeks as the effects of the storm reached far inland. New Jersey National Guard soldiers and airmen were active in support and rescue missions, including evacuations of residents as far north as Hoboken.

More New Jersey National Guard units were deployed overseas. The Public Affairs Detachment went to Guantanamo, Cuba; Headquarters and Headquarters Company of the 117th Combat Support Services Battalion was assigned to Kandahar Air Field, Afghanistan; the 508th Military Police Company to Kabul, Afghanistan; and the 250th Finance Detachment was sent to Kuwait. The state's Air National Guard continued its support of ongoing operations.

Newark native and entertainment superstar Whitney Houston was found unconscious in her bathtub at a Beverly Hills hotel and later pronounced dead at the age of forty-nine. Houston's death was ruled to be the result of drowning and the effects of heart disease and cocaine use. Her four-hour, invitation-only memorial service was held at the New Hope Baptist Church in Newark. Governor Chris Christie ordered flags around the state flown at half-mast in her honor.

## 2013

On February 3, Saint Stephen's Catholic Church in Kearny dedicated a monument to the four chaplains—Rabbi Alexander D. Goode, Reverend George Fox, Reverend Clark Poling and Kearny's Father John Washington—who gave their lives to save their fellow soldiers aboard the troop ship USS *Dorchester* on February 3, 1943.

On July 9, it was announced that a $25,000 grant from the Hudson County Open Space and Historic Preservation Trust Fund was approved to begin the restoration of Jersey City's bronze statue of Pieter Stuyvesant and return it to its original site. It was estimated that another $100,000 was needed to complete the project.

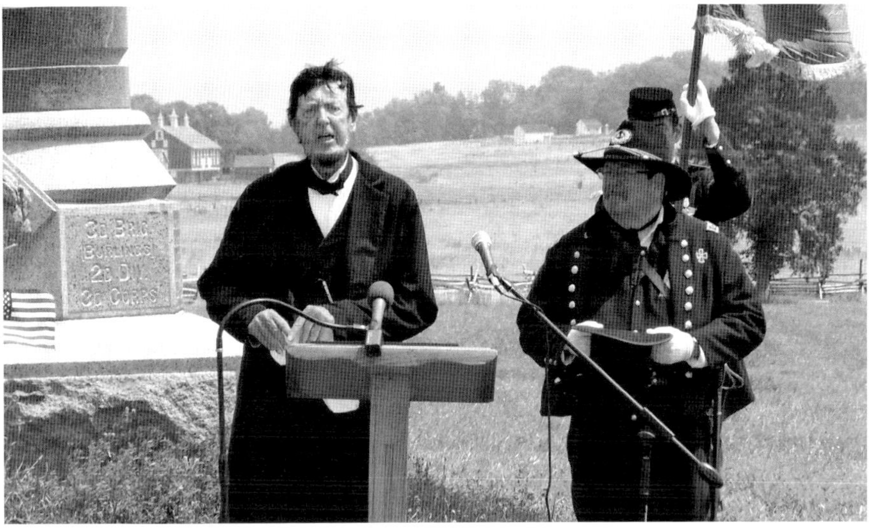


Bob Costello as Abraham Lincoln reads the Gettysburg Address as Elliot Stroul looks on during the New Jersey Civil War Sesquicentennial Committee's "New Jersey at Gettysburg Day" commemoration. *Bruce Sirak.*

"New Jersey at Gettysburg Day," an official rededication of the New Jersey monuments at Gettysburg Battlefield by the New Jersey Civil War Sesquicentennial Committee, was held at Gettysburg National Military Park on July 20.

The New Jersey Army National Guard's 150th Engineer Company was deployed to Kandahar Air Field, Afghanistan.

## 2014

New Jersey prepared to celebrate its 350th birthday as the most diverse state, with one of the most colorful heritages, in the union.

# Bibliography


Adelberg, Michael S. *The American Revolution in Monmouth County: The Theatre of Spoil and Destruction*. Charleston, SC: The History Press, 2010.

Barth, Linda. *A History of Inventing in New Jersey: From Thomas Edison to the Ice Cream Cone*. Charleston, SC: The History Press, 2013.

Bauer, K. Jack. *The Mexican War, 1846–1848*. New York: MacMillan, 1974.

Bilby, Joseph G. *Sea Girt, New Jersey: A Brief History*. Charleston, SC: The History Press, 2008.

Bilby, Joseph G., ed. *New Jersey Goes to War: Biographies of 150 New Jerseyans Caught Up in the Struggle of the Civil War, including Soldiers, Civilians, Men, Women, Heroes, Scoundrels—and a Heroic Horse*. Hightstown, NJ: Longstreet House, 2010.

———. *New Jersey's Civil War Odyssey: Untold and Long-Forgotten Stories of New Jerseyans and How They Coped with the American Civil War and Its Memory*. Hightstown, NJ: Longstreet House, 2011.

Bilby, Joseph G., and Harry Ziegler. *Asbury Park: A Brief History*. Charleston, SC: The History Press, 2009

———. *Asbury Park Reborn: Lost to Time and Restored to Glory*. Charleston, SC: The History Press, 2012.

Bilby, Joseph G., James M. Madden and Harry Ziegler. *Hidden History of New Jersey*. Charleston, SC: The History Press, 2011.

Bilby, Joseph G., and Katherine Bilby Jenkins. *Monmouth Court House: The Battle That Made the American Army*. Yardley, PA: Westholme Publishing, 2010.

Bilby, Joseph G., and William C. Goble. *Remember You Are Jerseymen: A Military History of New Jersey's Troops in the Civil War*. Hightstown, NJ: Longstreet House, 1998.

Bill, Alfred Hoyt. *New Jersey and the Revolutionary War*. Princeton, NJ: D. Van Nostrand, 1964.

Bisbee, Henry H., and Rebecca Bisbee Colesar. *Martha, 1808–1815: The Complete Furnace Diary and Journal*. Burlington, NJ: Henry H. Bisbee, 1976.

Blackwell, Jon. *Notorious New Jersey: 100 True Tales of Murders and Mobsters, Scandals and Scoundrels*. New Brunswick, NJ: Rivergate Books, 2008.

Bloomer, Lieutenant Colonel Edgar N. *Historical and Pictorial Review of the National Guard of the State of New Jersey*. Baton Rouge, LA: Army and Navy Publishing Company, 1940.

Bond, Gordon. *North Jersey Legacies: Hidden History from the Gateway to the Skylands*. Charleston SC: The History Press, 2012.

Braisted, Todd. *Bergen County Voices from the American Revolution: Soldiers and Residents in Their Own Words*. Charleston, SC: The History Press, 2013.

Buchholz, Margaret Thomas. *New Jersey Shipwrecks: 350 Years in the Graveyard of the Atlantic*. West Creek, NJ: Down the Shore Publishing, 2004.

Cooper, Jerry. *The Rise of the National Guard: The Evolution of the American Militia, 1865–1920*. Lincoln: University of Nebraska Press, 1997.

Cranmer, H. Jerome. *New Jersey in the Automobile Age: A History of Transportation*. Princeton, NJ: D. Van Nostrand Company, 1964.

Cunningham, John T. *Made in New Jersey: The Industrial Story of a State*. New Brunswick, NJ: Rutgers Press, 1954.

———. *Newark*. Newark: The New Jersey Historical Society, 1966.

———. *New Jersey: America's Main Road*. Garden City, NY: Doubleday, 1966.

———. *The New Jersey Shore*. New Brunswick, NJ: Rutgers Press, 1958.

———. *Railroading in New Jersey*. Newark: Associated Railroads of New Jersey, 1952.

———. *This Is New Jersey*. 3rd edition. New Brunswick: Rutgers Press, 1978.

———. *The Uncertain Revolution: Washington and the Continental Army at Morristown*. West Creek, NJ: Down the Shore Publishing, 2007.

Di Ionno, Mark. *A Guide to New Jersey's Revolutionary War Trail for Families and History Buffs*. New Brunswick, NJ: Rutgers Press, 2000.

Fabend, Firth Haring. *New Netherland in a Nutshell: A Concise History of the Dutch Colony in North America*. Albany, NY: New Netherland Institute, 2012.

Farrier, George H. *Memorial of the Centennial Celebration of the Battle of Paulus Hook, August 19, 1879, with a History of the Early Settlement and Present Condition*. Jersey City, NJ: M. Mullone, Printer, 1879.

Federal Writers' Project. *New Jersey: A Guide to Its Past and Present*. New York: Viking Press, 1939.

———. *Stories of New Jersey: Its Significant Places, People and Activities*. New York: M. Barrows and Company, 1938.

Fleming, Thomas. *New Jersey: A History*. New York: W.W. Norton, 1977.

Foster, James Y. *New Jersey and the Rebellion: A History of the Services of the Troops and People of New Jersey in Aid of the Union Cause*. Newark, NJ: Dennis & Company, 1874.

Fox, Tom. *Hidden History of the Irish in New Jersey*. Charleston, SC: The History Press, 2011.

Funnell, Charles E. *By the Beautiful Sea: The Rise and High Times of That Great American Resort, Atlantic City*. New Brunswick, NJ: Rutgers Press, 1975.

Gabrielan, Randall. *Explosion at Morgan: The World War I Middlesex Munitions Disaster*. Charleston, SC: History Press, 2012.

Gannon, Michael. *Operation Drumbeat: The Dramatic True Story of Germany's First U-Boat Attacks Along the American Coast in World War II*. New York: Harper & Rowe, 1990.

Gentile, Gary. *Shipwrecks of New Jersey*. Norwalk, CT: Sea Sports, 1988.

Gillette, William. *Jersey Blue: Civil War Politics in New Jersey—1854–1865*. New Brunswick, NJ: Rutgers, 1995.

Gordon, Thomas F. *Gazetteer of the State of New Jersey, Comprehending a General View of Its Physical and Moral Condition, Together with a Topographical and Statistical Account of Its Counties, Towns, Villages, Canals, Rail Roads, etc., Accompanied by a Map*. Trenton, NJ: Daniel Fenton, 1834.

Green, Howard L. *Words That Make New Jersey History*. New Brunswick, NJ: Rivergate Books, 2009.

Guernsey, R.S. *New York City and Vicinity During the War of 1812, Being a Military, Civic and Financial Local History of that Period*. New York: Charles L. Woodward, 1889.

Hickey, Donald R. *The War of 1812: A Forgotten Conflict*. Chicago: University of Illinois Press, 1989.

Hogarty, Richard A. *Leon Abbett's New Jersey: The Emergence of the Modern Governor*. Philadelphia: American Philosophical Society, 2001.

Jacobs, Jaap. *The Colony of New Netherland: A Dutch Settlement in Seventeenth Century America*. Ithaca, NY: Cornell University Press, 2009.

Karnoutsos, Carmela Ascolese. *New Jersey Women: A History of Their Status, Roles and Images*. Trenton: New Jersey Historical Commission, 1997.

Kennedy, Steele Mabo, et al, eds. *The New Jersey Almanac, 1964–1965*. Tercentenary edition. Upper Montclair: New Jersey Almanac, 1963.

Kull, Irving S. *New Jersey: A History*. 4 vols. New York: American Historical Society, 1930.

Lamb, Martha J. *History of the City of New York, Its Origin, Rise and Progress*. Vol. II. New York: A.S. Barnes & Co, 1880.

Lee, Francis Bazley, ed. *New Jersey as a Colony and State*. 4 vols. New York: Publishing Society of New Jersey, 1903.

Lender, Mark Edward. *One State in Arms: A Short Military History of New Jersey*. Trenton: New Jersey Historical Commission, 1991.

Lieby, Adrian C. *The Revolutionary War in the Hackensack Valley: The Jersey Dutch and the Neutral Ground*. New Brunswick, NJ: Rutgers Press, 1962.

Lockard, Duane. *The New Jersey Governor: A Study in Political Power*. New York: Van Nostrand, 1964.

Lossing, John Benson. *The Pictorial Fieldbook of the Revolution or, Illustrations by Pen and Pencil of the History, Biography, Scenery, Relics and Traditions, of the War for Independence*. New York: Harper & Brothers, 1881.

Ludlum, David M. *The New Jersey Weather Book*. New Brunswick, NJ: Rutgers, 1983.

Lundin, Leonard. *Cockpit of the Revolution: The War for Independence in New Jersey*. Princeton, NJ: Princeton University Press, 1940.

Lurie, Maxine N., and Marc Mappen, eds. *Encyclopedia of New Jersey*. New Brunswick, NJ: Rutgers Press, 2004.

Lurie, Maxine N., and Richard Veit, eds. *New Jersey: A History of the Garden State*. New Brunswick, NJ: Rutgers, 2012.

Mackenzie, Clyde L., Jr. *The Fisheries of Raritan Bay*. New Brunswick, NJ: Rutgers Press, 1992.

Mappen, Marc. *Jerseyana: The Underside of New Jersey History*. New Brunswick, NJ: Rutgers Press, 1992.

Martin, David. *New Jersey at Gettysburg Guidebook*. Hightstown, NJ: Longstreet House, 2013.

Martinelli, Patricia A. *True Crime: New Jersey.* Mechanicsburg, PA: Stackpole, 2007.

McCloy, James F., and Ray Miller Jr. *The Jersey Devil*. Wallingford, PA: Middle Atlantic Press, 1976.

McMahon, William. *Pine Barrens Legends and Lore*. Moorestown, NJ: Middle Atlantic Press, 1980.

McPhee, John. *The Pine Barrens*. New York: Farrar, Straus and Giroux, 1967.

Menzies, Elizabeth G.C. *Passage Between Rivers: A Portfolio of Photographs with a History of the Delaware and Raritan Canal*. New Brunswick, NJ: Rutgers, 1976.

Miers, Earl Schenck. *Down in Jersey*. New Brunswick, NJ: Rutgers Press, 1973.

———. *Where the Raritan Flows*. New Brunswick, NJ: Rutgers Press, 1964.

Miller, Pauline. *Three Centuries of Island Beach*. Toms River, NJ: Ocean County Historical Society, 1982.

Millman, Chad. *The Detonators: The Secret Plot to Destroy America and an Epic Hunt for Justice*. New York: Little, Brown and Company, 2006.

Mitnick, Barbara, ed. *New Jersey in the American Revolution*. New Brunswick, NJ: Rivergate Books, 2005.

Mitros, David. *Gone to Wear the Victor's Crown: Morris County, New Jersey and the Civil War, A Documentary Account*. Morristown, NJ: Morris County Heritage Commission, 1998.

New Jersey Historical Commission. *"Steal Away, Steal Away…": A Guide to the Underground Railroad in New Jersey*. Trenton: New Jersey Historical Commission, 1999.

Phillips Eaton, Harriet. *Jersey City and Its Historic Sites*. Jersey City, NJ: Women's Club of Jersey City, 1899.

Pierce, Arthur D. *Iron in the Pines: The Story of New Jersey's Ghost Towns and Bog Iron*. New Brunswick, NJ: Rutgers Press, 1957.

Pike, Helen Chantal. *Asbury Park's Glory Days: The Story of an American Resort*. New Brunswick, NJ: Rutgers Press, 2005.

Pomfret, John E. *Colonial New Jersey: A History*. New York: Charles Scribner's Sons, 1973.

Roberts, Russell, and Rich Youmans. *Down the Jersey Shore*. New Brunswick, NJ: Rutgers Press, 1993.

Sackett, William E. *Modern Battles of Trenton, Being a History of New Jersey's Politics and Legislation from the Year 1868 to the Year 1894*. Trenton: John L. Murphy, 1895.

Schmidt, Hubert. *Agriculture in New Jersey: A Three-Hundred-Year History*. New Brunswick, NJ: Rutgers Press, 1973.

———. *Rural Hunterdon: An Agricultural History*. New Brunswick, NJ: Rutgers Press, 1945.

Schwartz, Joel. *The Development of New Jersey Society*. Trenton: New Jersey Historical Commission, 1997.

Seguine-Levine, Joan. *Images of America: Perth Amboy*. Charleston, SC: Arcadia, 1996.

State of New Jersey Adjutant General's Report, Trenton. Trenton: State of New Jersey, various years, 1848–1929.

State of New Jersey. *Record of Officers and Enlisted Men of New Jersey in the War With Mexico, 1846–1848*. Trenton: State of New Jersey, 1920.

Stellhorn, Paul A. *New Jersey's Ethnic Heritage: Papers Presented at the Eighth Annual New Jersey History Symposium, December 4, 1976*. Trenton: New Jersey Historical Commission, 1978.

Stellhorn, Paul A., and Michael J. Birkner. *The Governors of New Jersey, 1664–1974*. Trenton: New Jersey Historical Commission, 1982.

Stinson, Robert R. *Hudson County Today: Its History, People, Trades*. Jersey City, NJ: Hudson Dispatch, 1914.

Studley, Miriam. *Historic New Jersey Through Visitors' Eyes*. Princeton, NJ: D. Van Nostrand, 1964.

Van Winkle, Daniel. *Old Bergen: History and Reminiscences with Maps and Illustrations*. Jersey City, NJ: John W. Harrison, 1902.

Veit, Richard, ed. *Digging New Jersey's Past: Historical Archeology in the Garden State*. New Brunswick, NJ: Rutgers Press, 2002.

Volkman, Ernest. *Espionage: The Greatest Spy Operations of the Twentieth Century*. New York: John Wiley & Sons, 1995.

Wacker, Peter O. *The Musconetcong Valley of New Jersey: A Historical Geography*. New Brunswick, NJ: Rutgers Press, 1968.

Weiss, Harry B. *The History of Applejack or Apple Brandy in New Jersey from Colonial Times to the Present*. Trenton: New Jersey Agricultural Society, 1954.

Weiss, Harry B., and Grace M. Weiss. *Rafting on the Delaware River*. Trenton: New Jersey Agricultural Society, 1967.

Wilson, Harold F., ed. *Outline History of New Jersey*. New Brunswick, NJ: Rutgers Press, 1950.

Winkler, John F. *Wabash 1791: St. Clair's Defeat*. Oxford, UK: Osprey, 2011.

Witcover, Jules. *Sabotage at Black Tom: Imperial Germany's Secret War in America, 1914–1917*. Chapel Hill, NC: Algonquin Books of Chapel Hill, 1989.

Wolff, Daniel. *4th of July, Asbury Park: A History of the Promised Land*. New York: Bloomsbury, 2005.

# About the Authors

Joseph G. Bilby was born in Newark, New Jersey. He received his BA and MA degrees in history from Seton Hall University and served as a lieutenant in the First Infantry Division in Vietnam in 1966–67. Mr. Bilby is retired from the New Jersey Department of Labor and is currently part-time assistant curator of the New Jersey National Guard and Militia Museum in Sea Girt, New Jersey, a member of the New Jersey Civil War Sesquicentennial Committee and a freelance writer, lecturer and historical consultant. He is the author, editor or co-author of seventeen books and over four hundred articles on New Jersey history and folklore and military history. Mr. Bilby has received the Jane Clayton award for contributions to Monmouth County, New Jersey history, as well as an award from the New Jersey Historical Commission for his contributions to the state's military history.

James M. Madden was born in Jersey City, New Jersey, and received his BS in marketing from Saint Peter's College. He is a political consultant who has contributed articles to many Civil War publications and projects, including the New Jersey Civil War Sesquicentennial Committee publications *New Jersey Goes to War* and *New Jersey's Civil War Odyssey*, as well as co-author of *Hidden History of New Jersey*. He is also a trustee and treasurer of the New Jersey Civil War Heritage Association and its 150th Anniversary Committee, treasurer of the Lincoln Group of New York and member of the Association of Professional Genealogists and Hudson County Genealogical and Historical Society.

Harry Ziegler was born in Neptune, New Jersey. He received his BA in English from Monmouth University and his MEd from Georgian Court College. He worked for many years at the *Asbury Park Press*, New Jersey's second-largest newspaper, rising from reporter to bureau chief to editor and managing editor of the paper. He is currently associate principal of Bishop George Ahr High School in Edison, New Jersey, and is co-author of *Asbury Park: A Brief History*, *Hidden History of New Jersey* and *Asbury Park Reborn*.